ANTICO FORNO ROSCIOLI

A ROMAN GASTRONOMICAL EXPERIENCE

To Stefano

ELISIA MENDUNI

ANTICO FORNO ROSCIOLI

A ROMAN GASTRONOMICAL EXPERIENCE

PHOTOGRAPHS BY
MAURIZIO CAMAGNA

GIUNTI

Text
Elisia Menduni

Foreword
Massimo Bottura

Photographs
Maurizio Camagna

Editorial Manager
Marco Bolasco

Graphic design, cover
Fabio Cremonesi

Page layout
Adriano Nardi

Editing
Sara Bettinelli, Micaela Vissani

Translation
Kosmos Traduzioni, Reggio Emilia

The Publisher would like to thank the Roscioli family for the photo on page 155.

The author would like to thank Giacomo A. Dente, Marco Amato, Vito Cinque, Arcangelo Dandini, Fabio Del Frate, Nazzareno Guidi, Fulvio Pierangelini, Galleria Lorcan O'Neill and Mama's Home, Roma.

www.giunti.it
www.piattoforte.it

Via Bolognese 165 - 50139 Florence - Italy
Piazza Virgilio 4 - 20123 Milan - Italy
First edition: June 2016
First reprint: December 2016

FSC
www.fsc.org
MISTO
Carta da fonti gestite in maniera responsabile
FSC® C016466

Printed at Lito Terrazzi srl, Iolo (Italy)

CONTENTS

Foreword

by Massimo Bottura

I grew up under the table where my grandmother would roll out pasta. The dish closest to my heart has always been my mother's tortellini, because when you're with your family, when you're with your friends, food takes on a completely different dimension, a dimension where affection and warmth are the things that truly matter.
At Roscioli I feel at home, I feel like I'm with family.
All my people – from the Canadian interns who arrived yesterday to the Korean who will stay in Italy for two months, to Taka, Davide, and Beppe who are the beating heart of our restaurant – all of them stop to eat at Roscioli when they are in Rome. But this, in the end, is understandable; the point is that they all go back as soon as they can. Maybe for lunch, often staying for dinner, as has happened many times. Because they feel at home. They feel like they're with family.

Pierluigi and Alessandro started in their family bakery and have created something around them that represents them, as if it were their "home". They have done so using the ingredients they would choose to eat and the dishes they give their own children, all the while surrounded by passionate young people who share the same philosophy.
I remember, about ten years ago, when Alessandro came to dinner here and tasted a pure Parmigiano Reggiano di Bianca Modenese – Parmesan produced from the milk of Modena white cows – he was so amazed that for days afterwards he bombarded me with messages, emails and phone calls trying to get his hands on this rare, magical cheese. I managed to deliver and he shared the experience with all the Roman foodies for whom Roscioli is a veritable landmark.

The best Amatriciana in Rome? The best Carbonara? The best Gricia? Hard to say for sure, but does it make any sense to ask? All too often we ponder this futile question.
The proof is in the pudding. All my chef friends, from all corners of the world, can't help but go back there when they pass through Rome.

Roscioli is the story of a family you'll meet as you sit at their table enjoying a lovely burrata accompanied by the best anchovies in the world and chatting with the ever smiling and helpful waiting staff, under the watchful eye of Giusy, or as you watch the bakery at work, or shake hands with Chef Nabil, who you won't be able to resist complimenting. As you feel at home like nowhere else.

Roscioli is in Rome. The Rosciolis are Rome.

Massimo

FORNO
HOTEL
HOTEL
VICOLO R.VIII
DEI
CHIODAROLI

MERCOLEDì
20 Bocconcini Semp.
20 MN olive
20 MN Noce
GRAZIE

ROME

A city made by the passing of the centuries, of layers, of wheat, light and colour.

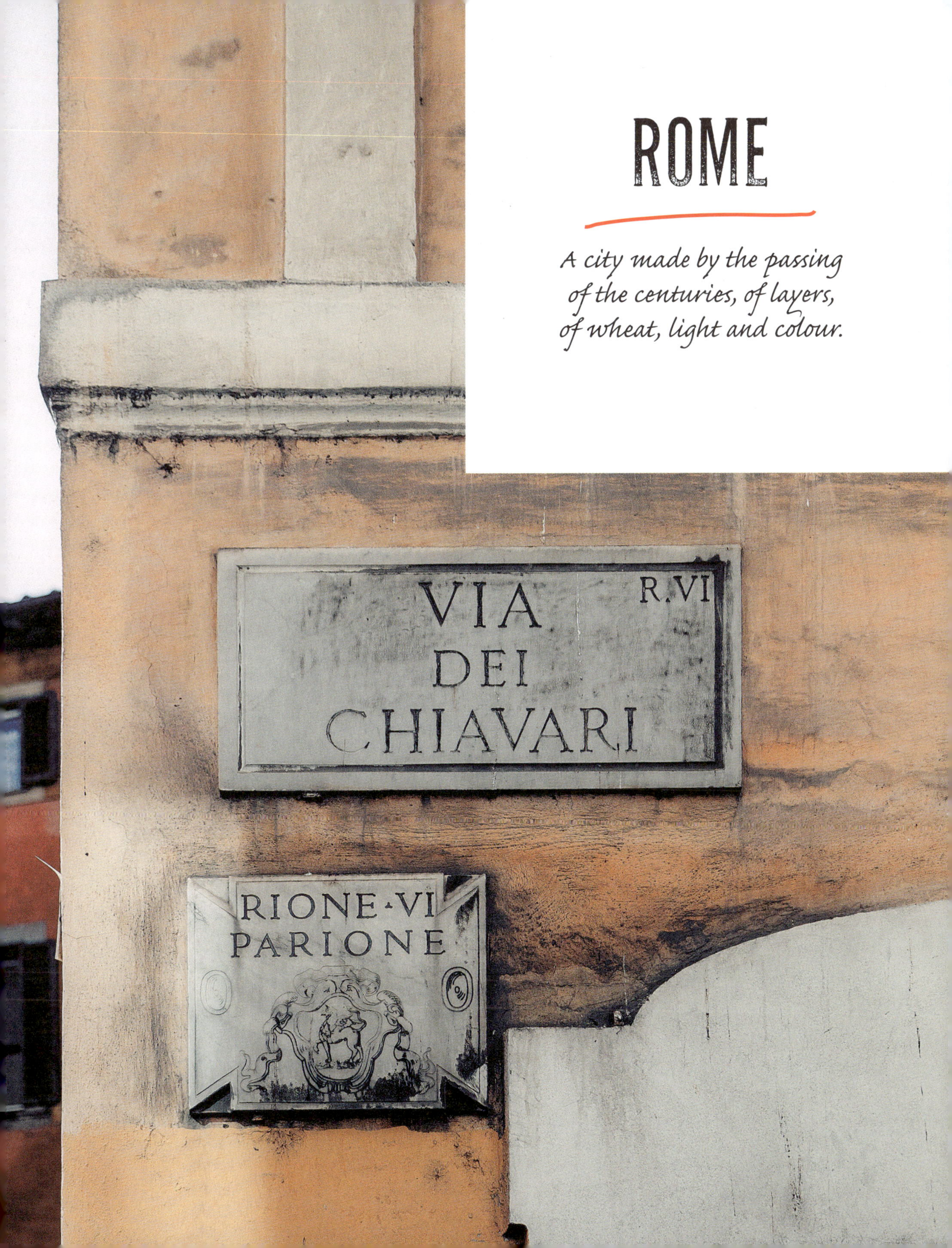

LOOKING UP, BEYOND

It's nice to look at Rome starting with the skies that tower above it and envelop it. They are not just any skies – they are clear skies, often scattered with clouds that would not be out of place in a sixteenth-century painting, they are crisp starry vaults, they burn orange-fuchsia during the languorous sunsets over the Tiber.

The light of this city is a continual transformation of incredibly ethereal, intense colours and atmospheres. Above, the light from the sky is dense and sinuous, elegant, clean and crisp; below, in the city, the light ricochets and reflects off walls, facades, archaeological excavations and shadows.

The city under this sky, a city born on a river, which went on to become the capital of an empire, is now a disorderly palimpsest of layered history. Dig downwards anywhere in the city and you will open up new archaeology and discoveries, glimpses into other eras and the wonderful, hidden recesses of history.

Strangely enough, this city was founded on a river, not on land.

The first inhabitants settled on Tiber Island, the only ford on the river at that time. It was on this stretch of the Tiber, not far from today's Ponte Rotto, that the road that transported salt from the sea to the mountains – which would soon come to be called the Salaria – crossed the route (the future Appian Way) that connected the North to the South and the Etruscans to the Greeks living in Cumae and Naples.

Between myth and history, when founding the city, Jupiter's consent had to be sought by means of haruspices. The sky and the flight of birds had to be studied in order to understand where to found the city: on the Palatine or the Aventine? That was the dilemma. On the 21st April over two millennia ago, the birds repeatedly veered to the north and the augur officiating the rite decreed the Palatine as the site of the city's foundation. Rome came into being by looking at the sky and this is no coincidence.

In the autumn, this original part of Rome is overtaken by incredible swarms of birds. The sky is invaded by thousands of starlings heading to Africa from North Europe, which dance madly alongside the traffic of the Lungotevere. These are not the vultures of old gliding in wide circles, but rather a strange and nervous contemporary iteration.

The Campus Martius was part of a vast marshy plain between the Tiber and the ancient walls of the Palatine, inside which the Palus Caprae (Marsh of the Goat) naturally formed. Initially outside the boundaries of the city, the Campus Martius spread over approximately two kilometres. Dedicated to the god Mars, it was used for military exercises and as a centre for trade for the populations who converged in Rome from the archaic period onwards. Due to a natural depression in the ground, the Campus frequently became flooded and covered with sand. It was green and very fertile. The lowest part of the marsh is where the Pantheon sits today.

Tarquinius Superbus, the last king before the Republic, took possession of the Campus Martius and had wheat planted there. Since we are going to talk about bread and wheat, it is a good time to mention the legend that says that during the uprising that led to the expulsion of this last king, Tarquinius, who was an arrogant and violent ruler, the sheaves of wheat in the Campus Martius were thrown into the river. This is how Tiber Island came to be. An island built on wheat.

55 BC saw the start of the monumental building work that transformed the Campus Martius area: Pompey had the first walled theatre in Rome erected, not far from where he had built his residence and his wonderful gardens.

Today, parts of the city still follow the Roman layout: all of Via del Biscione, Via dei Giubbonari, Via di Grotta Pinta, and Via dei Chiavari trace the perimeter of the auditorium, stage, and porticoes of the Theatre of Pompey exactly. Going to the underground floors of the Hotel Lunetta or those of the Da Pancrazio restaurant you can see real, tangible evidence. Columns, arches, and statues are nestled between the saunas of the hotel spa and the tables of the restaurant. The Theatre of Pompey extended all the way to Largo Argentina and you can still see the

S·BARBARA·V·M·SACR·

slabs of the many paved roads that were layered over one another over the course of two, history-rich millennia between the excavations, Roman-temple columns, and the cats of one of the chicest colonies in the capital.

This part of Rome is entirely built on about ten meters of rubble, topsoil and sand from the Tiber, which have obscured the past.

A past that today resurfaces flagrantly in every street, every building and every cellar. Via Arenula (or "fine sand") is built on sand residue left by the fickle Tiber which has burst its banks into the Campus Martius over the centuries. Today, it is part of the number 8 tram route, but it was once a maze of alleyways and towers. The lungotevere, the system of white, riverfront walls that offer protection from the recurring floods, would not be built until the 1800s, centuries later.

The main route for reaching the other side, Trastevere (the "Veii shore" named after the city of Veii, Rome's ancient rival), was the Ponte Fabricio. Paved with smooth travertine, the outline of its ship-like shape can still be seen clinging to Tiber Island.

la Feltrinelli
BESSO
UniCredit

There was no other stone-built bridge until Castel Sant'Angelo. Regola, Sant'Eustachio, Parione, Ponte: everywhere you turn, sooner or later you see the river, or hear it rushing by. It is a challenging river; otherwise why would the head of Roman paganism, and later Christianity, be called "Pontifex", the maker of bridges?

The same flowing water mirrored the long Medieval ages. This bend in the river hosts a triangle of houses and buildings built over ancient Roman ruins that is home to craftsmen, blacksmiths, innkeepers, and sellers of holy books and garments, as the street names remind us today: giubbonari (tailors), librari (booksellers), baullari (trunk makers), chiavari (key makers), canestrari (basket makers), leutari (lute makers). These were all artisans and tradespeople serving the pilgrims making penitent visits to St. Peter's.

On top of the pagan, republican, imperial, and medieval Rome, we can also add the splendour of the Renaissance and the Baroque period. This quarter, or rione (as the Roman *regiones* have been called since the thirteenth century), was inhabited by nobility, enclosed in their palaces and defensive towers, and formed the backdrop for the affairs of the most prominent families of Rome: the Cenci (Beatrice in particular), Capodiferro, Millini, Caetani, Borghese, Massimo...

We are now in the first half of the sixteenth century, a period in which the area starts to accumulate rich architecture and art treasures. At Palazzo Spada, Borromini innovates with forced perspective; at the Chancellery Bramante creates a stunningly elegant double colonnade with columns of red travertine that were originally found in the Theatre of Pompey. The imposing Palazzo Farnese is created by a whole battalion of *starchitects*: Antonio da Sangallo the Younger, Michelangelo, Vignola and Giacomo della Porta.

Vicolo dei Granari reminds us that this is a place where wheat has been conserved and bread made since time immemorial. The name Via Monte della Farina comes from Monte Frumentario, which was a Renaissance charity organisation and a kind of pawnshop. It accepted wheat and flour from bakers as collateral and gave loans in kind to the needy to save them from the loan sharks who were common even back then. It was in this very part of the city, possibly right in the

courtyard at the present day number 19, that Julius Caesar was stabbed to death at the foot of Pompey's statue. It was the Ides of March, the 15th of the month in 44 BC, and Caesar was 56 years old. A grandiose Latin inscription tells us so, without failing to mention the many taverns, which it deems "ignobles" – a term that needs no translation. There must have been a lot of rubbish around, judging from the many writings forbidding "far mondezzaro" – littering – and threatening implausible punishments.

Not far away there is also the large, white building of the Monte di Pietà, which was an actual bank, with three sumptuous and opulently decorated palaces which also show Borromini's hand. Around it, constantly observed by a stunningly beautiful bas relief depicting a weak Christ, there were – and still are – goldsmiths, watchmakers, and jewellers.

This corner of Rome just steps away from the Roman Ghetto, with its narrow streets that lead into the big, open space of the Campo de' Fiori, remains, at heart, the home of artisans. Campo de' Fiori is the only historic Roman square without a church, and perhaps this is no coincidence. Callistus III had it paved in 1456 (it was previously a field of flowers) and many palazzi were constructed nearby. In 1478, when the Campidoglio market was moved to the nearby Piazza Navona, inns, taverns, and refreshment stops appeared and the Campo de' Fiori became an important focal point in the affairs of the Renaissance city. It was

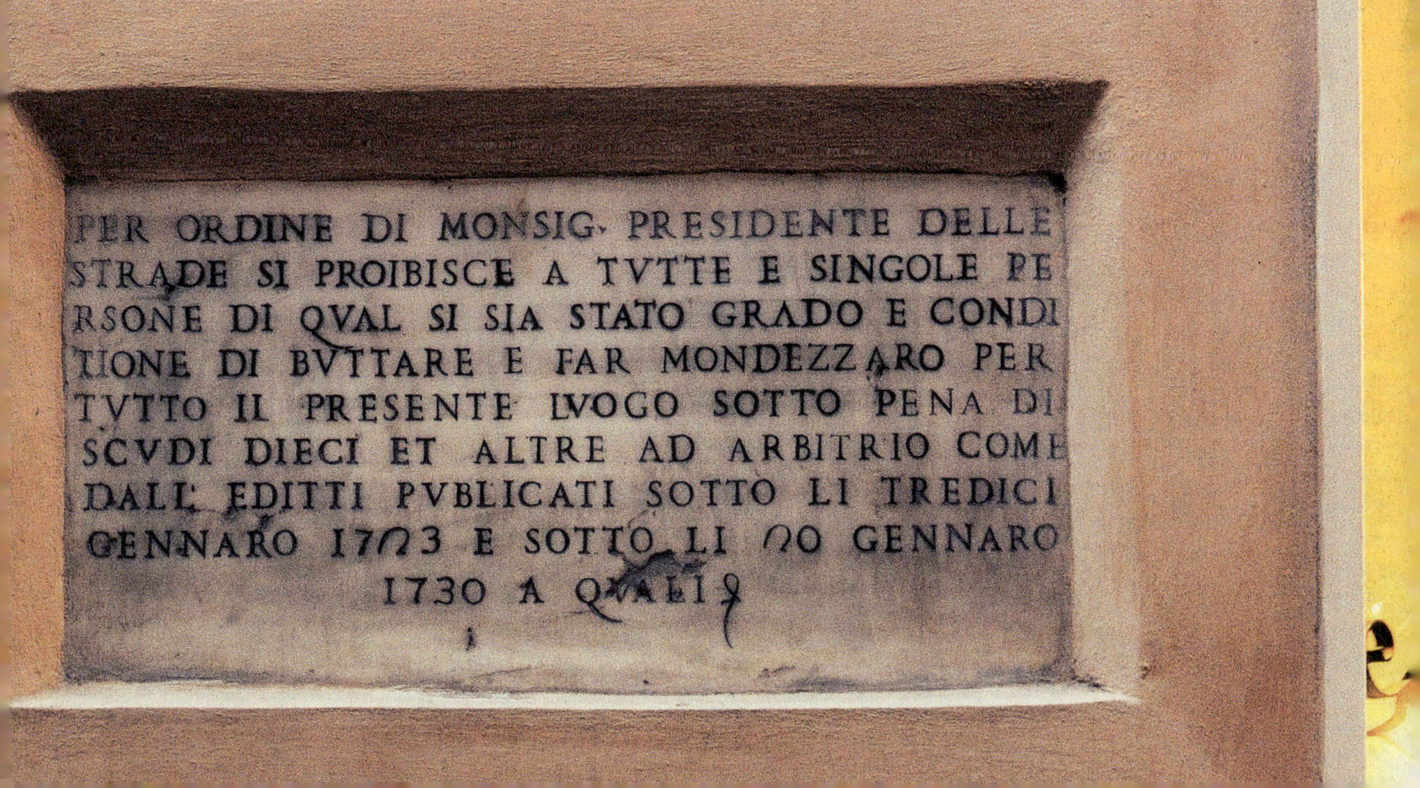

IOBAPTI

CLEMENS·VIII·PONT·MAX
MONTEM PIETATIS
PAVPERVM·COMMODO·INSTITVTVM
NE·CRESCENTIS·OPERIS·AVGVMENTVM
LOCI·PRAEPEDIRET·ANGVSTIA
EX·AEDIBVS·A·SIXTO·V·P·M·COEMPTIS
IN·HAS·AMPLIORES·TRANSTVLIT
ET·BENEFICIIS·AVXIT
ANNO·SAL·MDCIIII·PONTIF·XIII
PETRO·CARDINALI·ALDOBRANDINO
PROTECTORE
SPQR

here that popes and ordinary folk came together in matters of love, betrayals and marriages of convenience. It was here that the great Piazza Navona market was moved in the late nineteenth century and it was here that the peasants of the Pontine marshes would bring their carts of fruit and vegetables. It is also home to a bronze statue of Giordano Bruno, who stares, proud and wrapped up in his hooded Dominican habit, towards the Vatican that burned him in this very square in the year of our lord 1600.

Several black and white postwar movies tell us the story of this unique market. *Campo de' Fiori:* it's 1943. Anna Magnani plays Elide the fruit seller and Aldo Fabrizi is Peppino, the fishmonger. The director is Mario Bonnard but one of the screenwriters is a certain Federico Fellini. Soon, the Allied planes will come to bomb Rome, and the pair will meet again in *Rome, Open City*. But none of this has happened yet. For now, there is only the grace of a beautiful summer's day of a sort that we can still enjoy today – one of those days when the sun nestles between tall buildings and illuminates the narrowest streets.

Today the Campo de' Fiori market is at risk of losing its authenticity, becoming more of a tourist attraction than a real place for commerce. Some stands are little gastronomic jewels, others ornate displays of superb fruits and vegetables, but others only pay homage to quality. The real down-to-earth feeling of decades ago has disappeared.

The life of the square has followed the evolution of a neighbourhood that has changed completely from the post-war era to today. Once a working-class neighbourhood, a village within the city, it was in practice almost entirely pedestrian, since everyone extended their living rooms outward with tables and chairs in the courtyards and doorsteps. Clothes were washed in the street, Sister Medea "capava" – trimmed – artichokes, vineyard workers came on Fridays and people played cards. Romans still lived there.

Since the mid-1980s, a lot has changed. The houses in the centre have become finely-restored, upper-class residences. A "certain kind of Rome" has started to live in the neighbourhood, which, in a short space of time, has become an elegant area. Today the cobblestones of the old Campus Martius are traversed by judges of the Ministry or State Council, French ambassadors, cardinals and bishops, the Swedish Sisters of St. Bridget, intellectuals, the nouveau riche, students who crowd the few remaining bookstores and guides leading swarms of Japanese tourists.

RISTORANTE CUCINA ROMANA

FARNESE

THE BAKERY

A family of bakers comes to Rome from the Marche, bringing "goodness" to the bread making tradition of the capital. That is how the Forno Roscioli was born.

33
Roscioli

I WANT TO GO TO ROME

From the Marche region to Rome to escape the sheep and the countryside. Marco Roscioli chases his dream of escape – at full throttle – and plans his bakery.

Marco

June 1959. It's Sunday. We're in Rocca di Montemonaco, a small town scattered over the Monti Sibillini in the Marche region. Thirty houses, nestled between farms and forest, 1000 metres above sea level.

Marco is twelve years old and is going to see to the sheep as his father has asked him to do. He's been doing it since he started school. He's just finished his fifth year and has a summer spent herding his family's 42 sheep before him. The small flock, 8 cows, 2 mules, a field and a lot of hard work are the only things keeping the Roscioli family going. Luigi, Marco's father, settles his debts with the grocer every season from the lambs he sells at the town fair. His mother, Jolanda, makes cheese and shears sheep. This is how the Roscioli family survived the post-war period. There was no hunger, but there was no money either. Jolanda was a Roscioli even as a young girl, not just when she got married. There were five Roscioli families in the town and, over time, the genealogies had interwoven to form a single, sturdy family tree.

On that Sunday, while walking the path between the pastures and the farm, Marco cried for the whole afternoon. Even though he was small, he had already made up his mind: he did not want to be a shepherd. When he went home at sunset, his mother could see that Marco was unhappy and told her brother Umberto, who was visiting the town, that her little one dreamed about leaving for Rome.

For uncle Umberto, there was no problem "taking on" Marco at the bakery where he worked in Rome. If she was in agreement, Marco could leave with him, in the car, that very evening..

Marco was very excited. Bursting with happiness, he ran to his room to gather a few items of clothing in a bag before leaving for the capital with his uncle. He didn't have a lot of clothes, but he didn't forget his denim overalls, which had come from America.

There was just one problem. The next day Marco was to have his fifth year exam, the exam that would allow him to get into middle school. You can't throw away five years of education, said his mother: you have to finish school first. Then you can go to Rome. Uncle Umberto decided to stay. The next day he would go to the school, he would talk with the teacher, Franco, and he would convince him to give Marco a special exam that lasted one day instead of three. Thanks to the understanding of his teacher, Marco left for Rome that very Monday.

Uncle Umberto had a Giulietta with a Roma 39 number plate, he drove fast and loved cars, as all the Rosciolis do. Up at Scandarello Lake, on Via Salaria, he took a turn at speed, so fast that the two of them risked getting into a serious accident. But Marco wasn't afraid, he was happy and Rome was within his reach.

The Sixties

Rome is poorer than Marco expected.
Upon leaving the Marche region, Marco had dreamed about going to a big city, of becoming rich and getting a race car, but the city was hard and his job as a shop boy was arduous too. For seven months he didn't earn anything. He slept almost every night at the bakery, on bags of flour. He didn't have his own bed

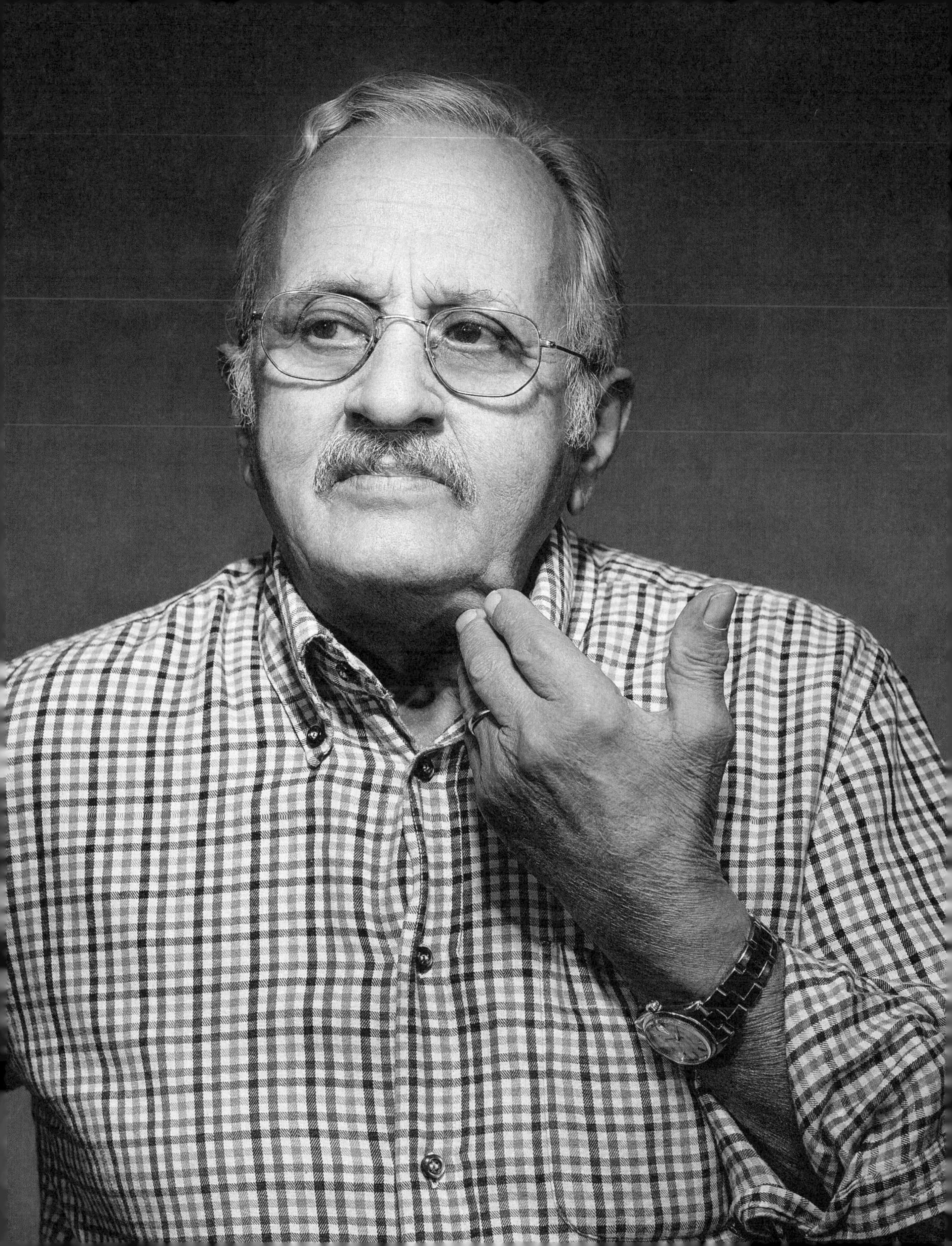

Roscioli
IL FORNO

and he worked constantly. His uncle saw to it that he ate and gave him work, but that was it. So Marco decided to write to his mother and tell her about his new life in Rome.
This letter was followed by correspondence between Jolanda and her brother, which led – after some prompting – to Marco's first salary: 500 lire.

There was no money in being a baker. Economic recovery had not yet begun and the price control on bread did not provide great returns. But there was enough to eat.

When he was fifteen Marco was kneading bread at his uncle Umberto's bakery in the Torpignattara area of Rome, behind the working-class suburb of Marranella. His uncle was not only his mentor in breadmaking but also in how to run a bakery. At the same time, he was getting his middle school diploma at night school and learning how to type.
At eighteen he left the suburbs and moved to Viale delle Medaglie d'Oro, to his uncle Franco's bakery, where he dedicated himself to making pizza dough.

Before leaving to join the military, Marco decided to buy a red Vespa 200 SS and go on holiday for fifteen days. The Vespa cost 387,000 lire, but it was the most beautiful Vespa in Rome. It was also his first ever holiday.

The first stop on his holiday was to visit his family, in Rocca di Montemonaco. This was only to last one day before he set off again for a roaring summer in Rimini and Riccione on the Adriatic Coast. Three kilometres from the town, on the way out of Rocca di Montemonaco, he noticed a black Fiat 1500 with a beautiful young girl inside. Marco knew that the car was going in the direction of his town, as the road didn't lead anywhere else, so he turned around and went back, hoping to meet this girl that already looked like a woman, despite the fact that she was only twelve years old. He followed the car on his Vespa and, upon arriving in the town square, met Rita. After his military service she was to become his wife.

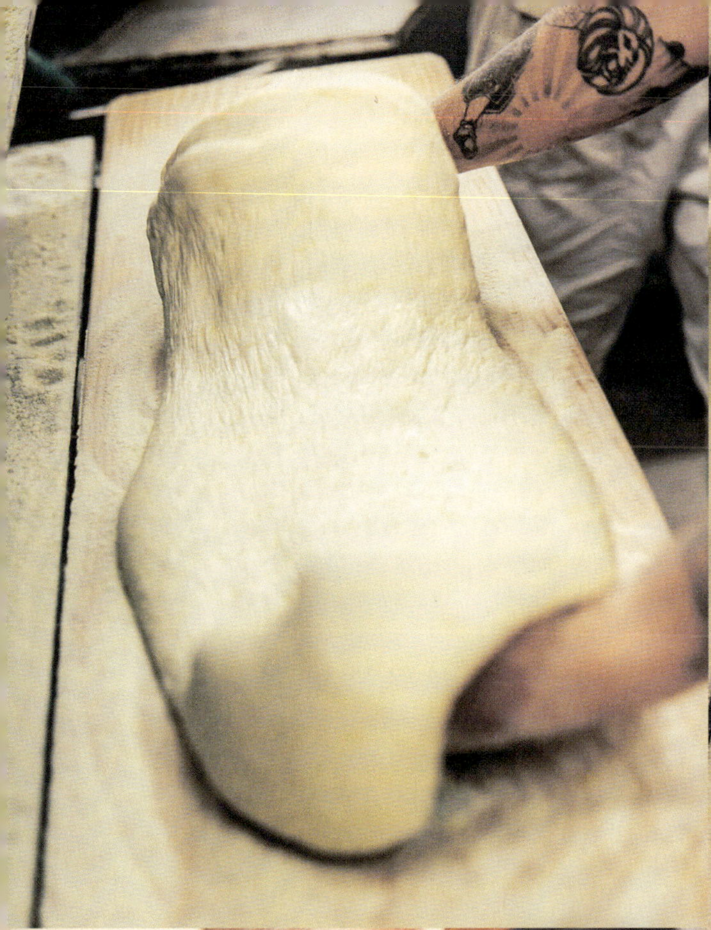

His military experience in the Air Force took Marco first to Bari, then to the Italian Air Force Academy in Pozzuoli, near Naples, where he was a waiter at the officers' club, and lastly to Ciampino. This was a stroke of luck for Marco: Ciampino Airport was not far from his uncle's bakery, where he would work when free from his military commitments. More importantly, it was close to the college where Rita was studying. There was another lucky turn of events: despite the fact he had been assigned to clean the planes in one of the airport hangers, thanks to his shorthand typing skills he was immediately promoted to the flight department office. He was a brilliant typist, while thanks to his expertise and technical skill with engines he was able to win over the Marshal and get himself assigned to a number of presidential flights.

This is how Marco came to be the steward for the Italian President. They would give him a kilo of coffee, a packet of MS cigarettes and a box of Charms sweets for every flight. Everything that was left over from the standard flight set up he would take and sell. He sold everything but the cigarettes, which would become one of his passions, along with cars.

He received 22,000 lire extra for every trip. An active, enterprising president, Giuseppe Saragat travelled a lot, and so Marco earned a lot. Over the entire course of his military career Marco racked up 700 flying hours, many of those spent taking the president to Sicily due to the 1968 earthquake in the Belice Valley. This earned him 515,000 lire, which he used to buy his first white Fiat 500.

Roscioli
Roscioli

PANE S
alle N
€ 10,00

Many other cars would follow: an Abarth 595, a Mini Cooper race car, four Alfas, two Delta Integrales, two Audis, a BMW 3000, and a Porsche. Many are still in the garage.

Franco

After the war, masses of butchers, confectioners, chefs and bakers arrived in Rome from the Marche, Abruzzo and Umbria regions. All of culinary central Italy converged in Rome.

Four of Marco's mother Jolanda's brothers moved to Rome to become bakers. Uncle Umberto had a large bakery in Torpignattara, in the suburbs, together with his brothers, while uncle Franco had a bakery in Via Venezia.

Franco was a tiny man, always dressed in a shirt and jacket, never with a speck of flour on him. He was a bread manager, but he never got his hands dirty with dough, just concerned himself with accounts, money, projects, loans, investments and sales.

In 1953 he left for the United States where one of his uncles had moved in the 1920s. His first stop was Kenosha, Wisconsin, a wealthy American province in the middle of nowhere where his uncle had opened a grocers.

Canada would follow. Then New York.

Franco was determined to discover new things in order to set himself apart on the Roman scene. He found soft bread in the States, like a brioche, without much of a crust and full of fat, which was not perishable, toasted easily and came in a standard, square shape. He could see that this kind of bread was interesting and, in its own way, revolutionary.

He returned to Rome with an expert Canadian baker and bought a machine on the black market the likes of which had never been seen before in Italy – an industrial bread slicer. This heavy piece of machinery came by boat the next month, arriving at the port of Naples, and he started making bread straight away. It wasn't the classic, sandwich bread of Piedmont, which was made with a lot of butter and had clear French origins, but rather the first American-style sliced bread ever seen in Italy.

For Franco it was too rich, too soft, too sweet, so he invented his own recipe, a version of Ferrarese sourdough adapted for making American-style white bread: water, flour, salt and plenty of lard, all of which underwent intensive kneading. The soft dough was split into two pieces of 2 kg, twisted and placed in box-like moulds. Rome was about to be invaded by sandwich bread. Franco opened three bakeries thanks to his success: one in Via Venezia, another in Via dell'Alberone and the third in Piazzale delle Medaglie d'Oro.

The Seventies

Marco and Rita were married on 7th May 1970. At the altar of the San Felice da Cantalice Church in the southern Roman suburb of Centocelle, you could almost count three of them. Alessandro would be born just a few months later. The newlyweds lived with Rita's mother and could not wait to find their own home and a start a new life.

Uncle Franco sold sliced bread all over Rome. Alongside the bread he sold all kinds of foodstuffs and oversaw a network of agents that worked for him. Marco was one of them. The "round" involved going to customers and attempting to sell bread, baked goods, cold cuts, milk, cheese and other foodstuffs.

Marco replaced an agent with 21 years of experience at his back who earned 100,000 lire a day. Marco was a whiz when it came to selling and he demonstrated this once again by earning 19 million in one year. Those at home didn't see him much, but work advanced: in 18 months he travelled 192,000 km by car, so much that he got a sore on his foot from the accelerator.

The money for a year's "round" was quickly used up: Marco and Rita spent 14 million lire buying a home and furnishing it. When, a little later, uncle Franco proposed a business deal – a bakery in Via dei Chiavari – Marco was extremely apprehensive because he only had one million lira left. However, with the guarantee of his uncle and a few promissory notes, the seller agreed to part with it.

The bakery, whose origins dated back to 1824, was literally a rat's nest. They were everywhere. Everything was dirty and covered in coal dust, not to mention in terrible condition. But there was a big oven: a three-chamber, brick-built Tibiletti with white tiles and a hatch for the coal. It took up a whole room on its own.

Uncle Franco had vision. The quarter would grow and the bakery was already well known for its pizza. Plus, as they say, "if the Roscioli family gets it into their head to succeed, they are going to succeed". That is why uncle Franco rented out his bakeries and decided to help his nephew get his new business off the ground. After all, Campo de' Fiori is Campo de' Fiori, he said. On 26th February 1971 the Forno Roscioli – Roscioli Bakery – opened at 34 Via dei Chiavari. The first day's takings amounted to 87,000 lire.

Despite their optimism and enthusiasm, the beginning was difficult. It was only in 1978, when all the start-up debts had been paid, that the bakery really got going. It went from making 10 kg of pizza a day to 20 kg, then 30 kg, using 50-60 kg of flour in a day. However, these were still the times of controlled bread prices in Rome. 100 grams of good bread were guaranteed to everyone at a low price. You could buy 1 kg of bread with 120 lire, even if labour cost 130 lire a kilo. In order to grow, the bakery began to expand its range and offered pastries, biscuits, rusks and tarts.

marco
Roscioli
IL FORNO

Rita

Deceptively dainty, the women in this story are in fact the sturdy pillars that have brought balance and a sense of calm to the erratic, hectic world of a business that is open 20 hours a day, 365 days a year.

Rita was born in Centocelle and lived with her grandmother. She was placed in a boarding school when she was six years old. She only has happy memories of her childhood and early youth: she loved studying, Rome was extraordinary, the month she spent in the Marche region in her mother's home town was carefree and Marco would come around on his Vespa to see her more and more often.

After she got married, Rita became a mother. Marco was consumed by his work, by his hectic life. He was closed off, authoritarian and everyday life became difficult. Rita lived a parallel existence with her children, who she raised with love and who she encouraged to study.

In 1983 she would take up a role in the family shop. The full complexity of a chaotic business would fall on her shoulders – some debt and many debtors, the difficulty inherent to a family-run business that included Marco's brother and sister, who were now part of the company, and a meddling mother-in-law. But Rita was a bulldozer and with the discipline and dedication she had learnt at her boarding school she was able, slowly but surely, to face every difficulty.

The Eighties

The neighbourhood begins to change, both in terms of its appearance and its identity. For the bakery this is when things really start to take off. Marco's brother and sister are working in the family business, which, by now, is well established, and Rita carefully manages the cash. register.

The bakery smells of bread, but there is also the scent of Dash detergent in the air. Shelves are set up in a corner and filled with various sundries: tins, biscuits, animal food, brooms and detergents. The *quintalato* is still in force, whereby bakers are paid per quintal of flour used in their bread dough. However, Marco decides to diversify his range. The bakery still makes price controlled bread, but prepares

olive oil rolls, Genoese focaccia and various kinds of pizza, not just the white and red varieties, as well as many kinds of biscuits and rusks.

A thriving relationship with the Jewish community begins to flourish during the eighties. The ancient ghetto in Portico d'Ottavia is a particularly wealthy area, in sociocultural terms, and the bakery does very well out of it. Thanks to their strict approach to the Kashrut dietary rules of the Jewish community the "Gentile" Roscioli family win the trust of the Chief Rabbi.

Marco takes everything on board and develops dough for challah bread, the bread of the Sabbath, and produces excellent Matzo bread, while his rolls can always be found at the parties and weddings in the Jewish community. It isn't simply a case of making bread according to certain rules, using certified ingredients and dispensing with the lard. It means doing so with the Rabbi's blessing. Every step of the breadmaking process is overseen by a representative from the community who certifies that the bread has been made in accordance with Kashrut rules.

Marco does not stop at just making bread. Over the course of eighteen years he would go on to develop an extensive network selling kosher-certified products.

Every month Marco would go to Milan in his Audi and buy everything he needed to supply the Jewish community from what was – at that time – the only merchant in Italy. Alongside him was the community representative, who was by this time a friend and travel companion. On his way back to Rome, he would stop in Brescia at the only kosher margarine factory of the time and load up around 200 kilos. Part of it was for the bakery, the rest was for two famous Roman patisseries: Linari and Bernasconi. In addition to margarine, Marco also dealt in ricotta and Pecorino cheese, and fresh pasta. Before long, the trade from Rome's Jewish community would become an important part of his business, quite aside from the bakery. The elimination of lard, and the "consecration" of differentiated bread production would become a feature of the breadmaking process.

The Dash and dog biscuits would prove to be less important.

Alessandro

Alessandro can't remember his father from when he was a child. Marco left at half four in the morning and returned at 9 in the evening. Every day. He was always working. There were no days of rest. He even worked on Sundays: he did his "little run", his quick deliveries of bread that had been kneaded Saturday night and baked Sunday morning to private customers, hotels and restaurants. It was a continuous loop, non-stop work and left a vacuum in the family that was hard to fill.

Alessandro was 8 years old when he took the tram by himself for the very first time. He went from Centocelle to Largo di Torre Argentina. He was almost a man now. When he got to the last stop, he got off and went to the bakery on foot. Marco called his son into his workshop and gave him a circular dough cutter to decorate the tarts, as if it were the most normal thing in the world. Alessandro became an assistant pastry chef without even realising it. He made no mistakes, even though it was his first day as a pastry chef, and he was proud of himself.

Marco was a tough father, a great worker who dedicated himself totally to his work. He would say over and over that there could be no empty time at the bakery spent doing nothing. He would remind Alessandro daily that nothing is owed and that everything comes from sacrifice.

Alessandro learnt everything, and quickly: he kneaded, decorated, sold at the counter and made deliveries on his bike. Always, every day, after school, and during holidays too. Always.

Cantarelli

Alongside the many difficult memories enclosed within the narrow walls of the bakery, there is one that has an almost prescient light.

Marco would buy Parmigiano and prosciutto in the Parma region. Every year he would set off with Alessandro to deliver a cheque of guarantee to the Parmigiano Reggiano Bank for the purchase of sixty wheels of Parmigiano. Capital in the form of cheese had to be prepaid and Parmigiano Reggiano producers wanted a pre-sales contract as a form of guarantee.

Marco would also stop off at Langhirano to choose from the sweet Parma Hams: he would select his hams one by one, plunging a horse-bone needle into each hanging thigh.

Sometimes, on the way back, he would stop at Samboseto da Cantarelli, a restaurant that was to leave its mark on Alessandro more than any other. His memory of it is clear: the first door opened onto a grocers selling various kinds of prosciutto and Culatello ham and a counter filled with almost everything you could think of, from soap to cigarettes. Peppino Cantarelli dressed like a lord from another time with his perfect shirt, braces and shiny shoes. Above Mr Cantarelli's head, and behind the counter, there were several lovely bottles lined up one after the other that Alessandro had never seen before: Burgundy wine and Champagne, not to mention outlandish whiskies.

Behind the second door, past the grocers, you arrived in a smart, sophisticated restaurant. Mirella, Peppino's wife, would cook cappelletti and tortelli pasta, clay baked guinea fowl, roasts and a wonderful rice savarin.

Something about that chaotic grocery shop full of pasta and tins, that counter with Culatello ham and mortadella sandwiches for truck drivers, that "gastronomic fairground" with adjoining kitchen and tables, struck Alessandro. So much so that a few years later he would open his own take on the grocery store with kitchen.

VINERIA
ROSCIOLI
SALUMERI

INGREDIENTS FOR 4 TRAYS OF PIZZA

- 1 kg strong flour (Italian 0 flour)
- 680 ml natural mineral water
- 100 ml whole milk
- 1 g fresh brewer's yeast
- 25 g salt
- 7 g malt
- 200 g durum wheat semolina to dust on top
- extra-virgin olive oil for the tray

PIZZA

Knead the flour with the milk then add 450 ml of water. If you can, knead by hand to give strength and elasticity to the dough. Knead vigorously and make various folds; this first dough should end up firm and elastic. Leave to rest for an hour. Put the dough in a kneading machine and add 230 ml of the remaining water, the malt and the yeast. Knead for at least 10 minutes on a medium setting. Place the dough, which should be elastic but sufficiently liquid, in a spacious container and leave to rest for between 7 and 12 hours at room temperature. If it's summer, find somewhere cool. Once this rising period is done, turn out the dough by turning the container over directly onto a surface that has been dusted with a little semolina, but don't pull it with your hands. Make several folds and divide it into pieces of around 250 g each. Leave them to rest for 30 minutes, then stretch each piece out in a well-greased tray. Press gently with your fingertips, until the pizza is fully stretched out. Cook at 260 °C (or higher if you have a more powerful oven) for 12-13 minutes. Once cooked, brush the pizza with a little oil using a soft-bristled brush to finish.

PIZZA ROSSA/RED PIZZA

- 1 kg pizza dough

FOR THE TOMATO SAUCE

- 1 kg peeled tomatoes
- 10 ml extra-virgin olive oil
- 10 g salt
- 1 g oregano
- extra-virgin olive oil for the tray

Blend all the ingredients together with a hand blender and leave to rest for 5-6 hours. Roll out the dough and use a wooden spoon to spread the sauce on the pizza just before you put it in the oven. Cook at 260 °C (or higher if you have a more powerful oven) for 15 minutes. Once cooked, brush the pizza with oil to finish.

INGREDIENTS FOR AROUND 10 CROCCANTELLE

FOR THE BIGA
(PRE-FERMENTED BREAD STARTER)

- 1 kg soft white flour (Italian 00 flour)
- 550 ml natural mineral water
- 1 g fresh brewer's yeast

- 500 g biga
- 250 g soft white flour (Italian 00 flour)
- 150 ml natural mineral water
- 15 g salt
- 2 g fresh brewer's yeast
- 200 g durum wheat semolina for dusting the worktop

CROCCANTELLE/CRISP FOCACCIA BREAD

To make the biga, knead the flour, the yeast and the warm water together vigorously by hand, firmly stretching the ball to help strengthen the gluten structure of the dough and make it more elastic and smooth. Fold it several times, until you get an elastic dough. Leave to rise for at least 12 hours. Put the risen biga in the kneading machine and add flour, salt, yeast and water, then knead on the slowest speed setting for 10-15 minutes. The dough should be firm, but not overly solid. Put the dough on a work surface, shape it into a ball and leave it to rise at room temperature for 2 hours. Divide the dough into pieces of around 100 g each, shaping each piece into as regular a ball as possible, and leave them to rise in this shape for another hour. Place the dough balls on a work surface dusted with a generous amount of durum wheat semolina and stretch them out until they are extremely thin. Line a tray with baking paper and lay out the flattened focaccia, brushing off the excess flour from one of the two sides. Arrange the focaccia on the tray with the side with the most flour downwards. Oil the focaccia lightly using a soft-bristled brush, sprinkle on a little salt, and cook at 260 °C for 10 minutes.

INGREDIENTS FOR 40 PIECES

1 kg wholemeal flour *	100 g golden sesame seeds
480 ml natural mineral water	20 g honey
150 g butter	15 ml extra-virgin olive oil
15 g salt	

PANE AZIMO/UNLEAVENED BREAD

Put all the ingredients in a planetary mixer and knead for around 10 minutes. It works better if the water is slightly warm and the butter is already softened. Leave to rest for an hour at room temperature, then roll out the dough until it is thin and prick it all over with a fork. Use a pastry wheel to cut rectangles or squares and place them on a greased tray or a tray lined with baking paper. Cook in a pre-heated oven, preferably above 220 °C, for 25 minutes.

* WHOLEMEAL FLOUR

Today you can find several kinds of enriched, blended and wholemeal flours on the market. But what does it all mean? Real wholemeal flour has undergone little processing and naturally includes parts of the grain kernel and germ in the mixture; it is a rich blend of storage proteins, fats and vitamins. This flour is much more delicate and more perishable than white flour, but it is undoubtedly healthier. Enriched flours, on the other hand, are refined flours to which bran or middlings have been added. In fact, the law states that flour is wholemeal if it has a level of ash (i.e. minerals) between 1.3 and 1.7%, even if these substances are not naturally found in the flour. Here's the trick to knowing if bread is truly wholemeal: it should not be basically white with brown specks, but should be the same, dark tone all the way through. To recognise wholemeal flour over industrial wholemeal preparations, on the other hand, you should try to sift it. If it separates easily, you can be sure that it isn't the real thing.

INGREDIENTS

1 kg organic, semi-wholemeal, extra-strong flour (Italian type-2 flour)

780 ml natural mineral water

150 g sourdough starter *

23 g natural salt *

PANE DI LARIANO
LARIANO BREAD

Put the flour, 550 ml of water and the sourdough starter into the kneading machine and knead, working the dough thoroughly until it is smooth and elastic. As soon as you have achieved this, add a splash of the remaining water and salt while kneading on speed setting 2. When you have finished kneading the dough, place it in a spacious container to rise for around 6-7 hours at room temperature. Empty the dough from the container onto a floured work surface, without touching it. Gently divide the dough into 750 g pieces. Use scales to help you. Gently stretch out the dough a little until you get an almost rectangular shape. Fold the right side horizontally over 1/3 of the dough, then fold the left side over 1/3 too. Repeat the process, but working at 90 °C to the first folds, folding the top edge inwards, then the bottom. Leave to rest for an hour on a kitchen towel coated with plenty of flour. Once the dough has risen, turn it over onto the tray so that the fold is facing up. Place in the oven at 260 °C, turning the heat down to 240 °C immediately and bake for 45 minutes.

* SOURDOUGH STARTER

250 g organic, semi-wholemeal, extra-strong flour (Italian type-2 flour)

2 potatoes (the skins only)

250 ml natural mineral water

Wash the potatoes and peel them. Keep the skins to one side and discard the flesh. Soak the potato skins in water at room temperature for 48 hours.
Strain the water off and mix it together with 250 g of flour. Once you have a creamy mixture, pour it into a jar covered with a tea towel and leave it to prove in a cool place for 24 hours. After a day the creamy mixture will be thick, with a few fermentation bubbles on the surface. The sourdough should be refreshed everyday: remove 100 g of the starter and replace it with a mixture made with 50 g semi-wholemeal flour and 50 ml warm water. On the third day, remove 150 g of the dough and refresh it with a batter made of 75 g flour and 75 ml warm water. Keep refreshing it in this way until the creamy sourdough has doubled in volume and starts to give off an acidic smell, which is very similar to that of goat cheese. From this point on, keep the starter at room temperature for 4 hours a day and 20 hours in the fridge at 4 °C in a jar with a tight fitting lid. Refresh daily, combining 100 g sourdough with 200 g flour.

* NATURAL SALT

For years they focused on flour and yeast, without thinking too much about salt, say the Rosciolis. Then one day Francesco, a good friend who travels a lot, brought them some natural French salt that was raw, grey and slightly humid. They tried it and noticed a striking improvement in their dough preparations. Raw salt, which has not been bleached or had stabilisers added to it, is a living substance and interacts perfectly with the yeasts in their sourdough. While commercial salt is made up of 98% sodium chloride, meaning sodium and chlorine and very few other mineral residues, in natural sea salt "living" iodine is mixed naturally with the salt crystals (and is not added artificially, as occurs in iodised salt) and also contains calcium, magnesium, potassium, iron, copper, fluoride, manganese, zinc and many other minerals in smaller quantities.

INGREDIENTS FOR AROUND 50 MINI PIZZAS

FOR THE BASIC DOUGH	FOR THE BLOCK OF BUTTER	FOR THE TOMATO SAUCE
700 g strong flour	1000 g butter	500 g peeled tomatoes
420 ml natural mineral water	300 g flour	10 ml extra-virgin olive oil
20 g salt		5 g salt
20 g sugar		1 g oregano

PIZZETTE/MINI PIZZAS

Prepare the basic dough by dissolving salt and sugar in cold water. Make a well with the flour and pour the water in the middle. Knead the dough vigorously until it becomes smooth, elastic and even. Wrap the dough in cling film and place it in the fridge for half an hour.
Now is the time to prepare the block of butter: mix the softened butter together with 300 g of sifted flour, then spread the mixture out between two pieces of baking paper, making a rectangular shape, and place it in the fridge for at least 20 minutes. Roll the basic dough out into a rectangular shape that is thick around 1-2 cm. At this point, fold it in three. In other words, take the two opposite sides and fold them in towards the centre, without overlapping them. Let the mixture rest in the fridge, covered in cling film, for an hour.
Place the dough on a floured surfaced and use the rolling pin to roll it out, extending it lengthways and widening it slightly. When you have a fine rectangle, place the block of butter in the centre of the dough. Then take the two sides and fold the dough, first towards the centre and then in on itself (folded in four).
Leave to rest in the fridge for another hour.
Roll out the dough and cut disks of around 6-7 cm in diameter using a dough cutter.
Place them on a tray lined with a sheet of baking paper, taking care to leave a few centimetres between them, and leave to rest for another 30 minutes. While they are resting, place all the ingredients for the tomato sauce in a large pot. Cook from cold, without sautéing.
As soon as the sauce begins to boil, blend it all together carefully with a hand blender. Leave it to cook for another 15 minutes over a low heat.
When the mini pizzas have risen, use the index and middle finger of each hand to press down in the centre of each disk, creating a hollow into which you will add a spoonful of sauce.
Bake in the oven at 250 °C per 13 minutes.
Once cooked, brush with some oil using a soft-bristled brush.

INGREDIENTS FOR 4/6 PEOPLE

250 g puff pastry	5 g nutmeg
400 g fresh spinach	fine salt
200 g Parmigiano Reggiano	black pepper
400 g ewe's milk ricotta	coarse salt
2 eggs	1 egg to finish

TORTA PASQUALINA/EASTER PIE

Boil the spinach in water with a generous helping of salt. Once the leaves are tender, drain them carefully and leave to cool. Take the ricotta and remove as much of the whey as you can. You can wring it out in a linen cloth until the whey has drained and the cheese is dry. Chop the spinach on a cutting board and place it in a bowl. Stir in the ricotta with the grated Parmigiano, the nutmeg, the lightly beaten eggs and the salt and pepper. Roll out the puff pastry and spread it over a baking tray that has been well greased, including the sides; take care to keep a dozen strips of pastry to one side. Fill the pie with the ricotta and spinach mixture. Arrange the strips of puff pastry on top, weaving them together as if it were a tart, and brush the top with egg that has been diluted with a little water. Cook in the oven at 220 °C for 40 minutes. You can also try this savoury pie with other fillings: speck ham, ricotta and smoked Provola or ricotta, egg, mushrooms and Taleggio cheese.

INGREDIENTS FOR 10 BURRELLE

- 1 kg soft white flour (Italian 00 flour)
- 100 g margarine
- 40 g sugar
- 5 g fresh brewer's yeast
- 400 ml natural mineral water
- 1/2 glass of whole milk

FOR THE BRINE

- 180 ml extra-virgin olive oil
- 150 ml natural mineral water
- salt
- rosemary
- white onion soaked in milk

BURRELLE/OILY FOCACCIA BREAD

Dissolve the yeast in a little milk. Combine all the ingredients together in the kneading machine and start to knead. Pour in the cold water gradually. Thoroughly work the mixture until you have an even, soft and elastic dough. Shape it into a ball and leave to rest for an hour. Roll out the dough on a lightly floured work surface. Grease a tray around 40 cm in diameter and spread out the dough, pushing it down with your fingertips. The *burrelle* that are served at the *Forno* come in individual portions, and so are made in small moulds that are 10 cm in diameter. Press the tip of your finger firmly into the surface of the dough to create the classic "eyes" that this soft, oily focaccia bread is known for. Mix the oil with the water, add a pinch of salt to make a briny mixture and brush it generously over the focaccia. The "eyes" will fill with brine and will remain soft and liquid when baked. Leave the focaccia to rise in a tray at room temperature for another hour, then bake in the oven at 190 °C for 15-20 minutes. If you like, you can also add rosemary or lots and lots of finely chopped white onion that has been soaked for 1 minute in milk, spread in such a way so as to cover the entire tray.

INGREDIENTS

1 kg strong white flour (Italian 00 flour)	15 g almond paste
500 ml natural mineral water	10 g salt
250 g proved natural yeast *	the skin of 1 lemon
15 g cane sugar	380 g dried figs
90 g butter	250 g shelled walnuts

PANE AI FICHI/FIG BREAD

Put the flour, water and natural yeast into the kneading machine and work it well for 8 minutes. Add all the other ingredients, starting with the sugar and finishing with the dried figs and walnuts. Mix it all together on speed setting 1. When the dough is solid, shape a ball and leave it to rest in a warm place for 90 minutes. At this point divide the dough into two baguette-shaped loaves and leave them to rise for another 90 minutes.
Bake at 180 °C for around 50-60 minutes, one loaf at a time.

* MOTHER DOUGH AND SOURDOUGH STARTERS

This starter is a doughier version of the creamy, natural-yeast pre-ferment described on page 84. To make it you need to refresh half of the pre-ferment with double its weight in flour, the same kind that you will use to make the dough later, and knead it on speed setting 1 until you get a smooth and well-formed mixture. To refresh the sourdough starter, you have to give it a "daily soak" to remove excess acidity (around 3 litres of water at 20 °C with 6 g of sugar per every kilo of yeast), cutting the dough ball into little cubes and leaving them to soak for at least 20 minutes. When they have finished soaking, drain and knead them together with the same weight in flour if you are going to use the starter straight away, or with two times the dough's weight in flour if you have to keep it. The yeast that you are to use that day must be left to rest for at least 3 hours at 28°C before you use it. Cover the yeast that you are going to keep for the next day with a linen cloth and store it at 4-8 °C for around 18-20 hours.

INGREDIENTS FOR AROUND 20 OSSI OR 50 TOZZETTI BISCOTTI

1 kg pizza dough
→ *recipe on page 78*

200 g durum wheat semolina to dust on top

OSSI E TOZZETTI
BONES OF THE DEAD AND HAZELNUT BISCOTTI

Once the pizza dough has risen for 12 hours, turn it out by turning the container straight onto a work surface that has been dusted with a little semolina. Fold the dough several times, then divide it into small pieces. Fold the pieces lengthways and roll them in your hands, making long rolls around 4-5 cm in diameter. Place all the rolls on a tray with baking paper and cut into 8 cm-long pieces, if you want to make *Tozzetti* biscotti, or 20 cm-long if you want to make *Ossi* biscotti. Bake for 12-15 minutes at 260 °C.

PIZZE

INGREDIENTS FOR 2 PIZZAS

- 600 g strong flour
- 8 eggs
- 500 ml whole milk
- 350 g medium-aged Provolone, cubed
- 150 g Pecorino Romano
- 150 g Parmigiano Reggiano (aged 24 months)
- 100 g lard
- 50 ml extra-virgin olive oil
- 1 g fresh brewer's yeast
- 20 g sugar
- 8 g salt
- 8 g black pepper
- 1 egg yolk for the glaze

PIZZA AL FORMAGGIO/CHEESE PIZZA

Mix 500 g of flour and 250 ml of milk in a bowl, using your hands if possible. Knead for 5 minutes and shape an elastic ball that you will leave to rest for 12 minutes. Take the ball and add 250 ml of milk and 1 g of yeast and knead until you get a soft, slow-leavening dough. Cover the bowl with cling film and leave it to rest overnight. Finely grate the Pecorino and the Parmigiano; cut the Provolone into 1 cm cubes. Mix the dough with all the other ingredients, except for the Provolone, in the kneading machine and work it for 5 minutes. Add the Provolone and knead until all the cheese is mixed into the dough. Overturn the dough onto a floured work surface, then knead quickly to shape a ball and leave to rest for 20 minutes. Place the pizza dough with the smoother part facing upwards in a greased, high-sided, cylindrical mould that has been lined in baking paper or, if you can find it, use a paper mould for panettone. Brush the top of the pizza with the beaten egg yolk. Leave to rise for approximately two hours: the dough should rise to almost reach the top edge of the mould. At this point, put the cheese pizza in a pre-heated oven at 190 °C and cook for 45 minutes. For best results, spray a little cold water in the oven before putting the pizza in and place a bowl filled with water on a lower shelf. Once it has cooked, transfer the pizza to a cooling rack to cool.

INGREDIENTS

- 500 g soft white flour (Italian 00 flour)
- 200 g sugar
- 4 eggs
- 250 ml extra-virgin olive oil
- 250 ml whole milk
- the zest of 1/2 lemon
- salt
- 16 g baking powder for desserts
- cane sugar for decoration

CIAMBELLONE/RING CAKE

Work the eggs together with the sugar in the kneading machine until you get a pale, airy mixture that just about holds its shape.
Add the salt, oil, milk, lemon zest and, last of all, the sieved flour. Knead at a brisk speed for 2 minutes, then add the yeast. Knead it vigorously again for 4-5 minutes. Grease a ring mould and flour the sides. Pour in the dough, sprinkle some cane sugar on top and put in the oven. Bake at 180 °C for 20 minutes then at 160 °C for another 20 minutes.

THE MOULD

The secret to this ring cake lies in the shape of the mould. It doesn't matter if you whisk the egg whites separately, it doesn't matter if you gently mix the ingredients together... It's all about the shape, and consequently, the baking temperature: the same mixture, in a different mould, will give a different result.
Choose a narrow, deep mould made from aluminium for this recipe, rather than a wide, shallow one. Look for a customised mould, in other words, one that is narrow and deep, but – more than anything else – one that is closed in the centre; if you can't find one, ask a tinsmith to make it for you (as they used to do once upon a time). The fact that the heat is trapped in the centre by the covered hole will increase the temperature, channelling heat to the centre, shortening the baking time and thus making the *ciambellone* moister.

TORTA SOFFICE DI MELE / SOFT APPLE PIE

- 1 kg ciambellone mixture
- 4 apples: Rennet, Granny Smith or Monti Sibillini pink apples
- lemon
- cane sugar for decoration

You can also make a classic apple pie with the ciambellone mix. Peel the apples, remove the core and cut them into thin slices. Rinse them with water and lemon juice and dry them. Grease and flour a deep cake tin on all sides. Pour in 2/3 of the mixture and make the first layer of apple slices. Pour 1/3 of the mixture and make a second apple layer. Bake at 180 °C for 20 minutes and at 160 °C for another 20 minutes. Once baked, spread a little cane sugar on the top of the cake and put it back in the oven for another 2 minutes: the cake will come out looking glossy and delicious.

INGREDIENTS

- 1 kg plain flour (Italian 0 flour)
- 500 g sugar
- 350 ml dry red wine
- (traditionally Olevano Romano wines are used)
- 430 ml extra-virgin olive oil
- 25 g baking powder for desserts
- 20 g aniseed

CIAMBELLINE AL VINO/SWEET WINE PRETZELS

Pour the wine, oil, 350 g of sugar, the baking powder and the aniseed into a mixing bowl. Mix it all together thoroughly using a fork or a whisk until the baking powder has dissolved, then add the sieved flour gradually. You will end up with a rather soft dough, which you should knead as little as possible. Move the dough onto a lightly-floured work surface and knead until you get a smooth dough that is not sticky. Make little rolls of around 1/2 centimetre in diameter, then cut them to form 7-8 cm-long tubes.

Use your hands to connect the two ends of the tube and squeeze to close the pretzel. Dip one side of the pretzel into the remaining sugar. Lay them down on the other side on a tray that has been lined with baking paper. Place in a pre-heated oven at 220 °C and bake for 20 minutes.

INGREDIENTS

- 1 kg Viterbo hazelnuts
- 1 kg sugar
- 400 g egg white
- salt
- extra-virgin olive oil

BRUTTI MA BUONI/UGLY BUT GOOD BISCUITS

Toast and roughly chop the hazelnuts until you get rather fine, yet uneven, crumbs. Beat the egg whites until stiff, adding a pinch of salt, but making sure that they don't become too stiff. Mix the sugar with the chopped hazelnuts in a large bowl. Add the whisked egg whites and mix until you get an even mixture. Pour the mixture into a pot with a thick bottom (at least 2 cm), all the better if it is made of copper, and cook for 10 minutes over a low heat. Stir the mixture thoroughly until it reaches 45 °C. You'll know that the mixture is ready when you try to touch it with two fingers and it forms elastic, but not sticky, strings. At that point, move the mixture onto a lightly-greased work surface, marble where possible. Take a spatula and stir the mixture slowly to cool it. When it is almost cool, put it in a pastry bag. Cover a tray with baking paper and pipe out tufts of around 4-5 cm in diameter onto it. Bake at 150 °C for around 25 minutes or until the *brutti ma buoni* are golden.

BRUTTI
MA
BUONI

INGREDIENTS

- 1.2 kg soft white flour (Italian 00 flour)
- 500 g butter
- 500 g sugar
- 250 g almonds
- 6 eggs
- 20 g baking powder for desserts
- the zest of 1/2 lemon
- 1 vanilla pod

TOZZETTI/TOZZETTI BISCOTTI

Beat the eggs and the sugar in a bowl until the mixture starts to hold its shape and lighten in colour. Add the soft butter, the yeast, the grated lemon peel and the vanilla seeds. Toast the almonds and add them whole to the mixture. Add the sieved flour little by little, mixing well and kneading the mixture until it becomes even and soft. Move the mixture onto a floured work surface and use your hands to create wide baguette shapes that are 5 cm wide and 15-20 cm long. Place the baguettes in a tray that you have previously covered with baking paper and bake for around 20 minutes at 220 °C. Remove the baguettes and, while they are still warm, cut them into slices around 2 cm thick. At this point, put the *Tozzetti* back in the oven, then turn them over so that they become crisp on both sides. Take them out of the oven and leave to cool. *Tozzetti* biscotti last a long time if kept in airtight jars.

INGREDIENTS

FOR THE SHORTCRUST PASTRY

- 400 g soft white flour (Italian 00 flour)
- 500 g peeled almonds
- 180 g butter
- 150 g granulated sugar
- 2 egg yolks + 1 whole egg
- 1 vanilla pod

FOR THE FILLING

- 250 g ewe's milk ricotta
- 250 g sour cherry preserve *
- 60 g icing sugar
- sour cherries for decoration

CROSTATA DI RICOTTA E VISCIOLE
RICOTTA AND SOUR CHERRY TART

Put the ricotta to one side to drain the whey. It is important that it is extremely fresh. If you can see that the ricotta contains a lot of liquid, place it in a clean tea towel and gently wring it out. Toast the peeled almonds and chop them very finely into a sort of flour. Make the shortcrust pastry: knead the almond flour and the soft white flour together using your hands, with the granulated sugar, the butter, egg yolks, the egg and the vanilla seeds. Shape the dough into a ball and wrap it in cling film. Leave it to rest in the fridge for at least 30 minutes. Meanwhile, push the ricotta through a sieve, then work it together with the icing sugar in a large bowl to get a smooth, even mixture. Grease and flour a cake tin with high, tapered sides (at least 3-4 cm high), spread out the shortcrust pastry and lay it on the bottom of the tin, making it stick to the edges by pressing down lightly with your fingers. Cut the excess pastry and put it to one side. Spread a layer of sour cherry preserve on the bottom, then gently pour the mixed ricotta over the top and spread it with a teaspoon to get an even layer that is at least 2 cm thick. Use the remaining pastry to create strips and place them over the ricotta, criss-crossing them to create a weave. Bake in a pre-heated oven at 170 °C for 30-40 minutes.

* SOUR CHERRIES

Sour "Visciole" cherries, including Marasca and black cherries, are the acidic, "ugly sisters" of sweet cherries. From a botanical perspective, they are different species. The acidic, sour cherry belongs to the Prunus cerasus family, while the large, fleshy sweet cherry is the fruit of the Prunus avium, a much larger tree which, however, yields less fruit. For this recipe we recommend a sour cherry preserve that is made with whole fruits, which will be fleshier and crunchier, as well as tangy and sweet. If you can't find one, replace it with a regular sour-cherry jam, but not sweet-cherry jam: the note of tartness would be lacking, which is what this historic Jewish tart hinges on.

INGREDIENTS

- 1 kg Monte Amiata chestnut flour
- 1 l whole milk
- 1 l extra-virgin olive oil
- natural mineral water
- 700 g milk-soaked raisins
- 100 g pine nuts
- 50 g sugar
- 4 g bicarbonate
- salt

CASTAGNACCIO/CHESTNUT FLOUR CAKE

Mix the chestnut flour together with the sugar, salt, bicarbonate, milk and oil until you get a smooth, even mixture. Adjust the density with warm water. Remember that the mixture should never be firm, but rather soft and almost liquid. Carefully grease a baking tray with low sides (maximum 2 cm) and pour in the mixture. Add the soaked raisins, making sure they are completely dry, and the pine nuts. Bake in the oven at 200 °C for 20 minutes.
If you notice that it swells up when baking, pierce it slightly with a skewer to let the steam out. Serve hot or warm.

THE DELICATESSEN WITH KITCHEN

Evolution by design replaces evolution by chance.

€ 150,00 AL KG

UTTER PLEASURE

The format of a Delicatessen with an adjoining kitchen is designed around the idea of extreme, sophisticated and all-encompassing culinary pleasure. Pleasure and nothing else.

The nineties

The neighbourhood had changed for good. There was nothing left of old peasant Rome. The houses were now all inhabited and the small shops had all become fashion boutiques. One Saturday afternoon, at the beginning of the nineties, the Forno Roscioli baked 120 red pizzas, each 1.70 metres long. It was a nice record, not to mention an extremely satisfying one. The bakery closed at lunchtime and, instead of enjoying a few hours break, Marco and his sons made ring cakes and tarts. Francesco Coda, a pastry chef from Gragnano, rounded out his pension by helping in the store. Many of the details now found in many of the bakery's pastry recipes can be traced back to his hands and his craft as an aromistiere, or, in other words, as an expert of patisserie essences.

The ring cake recipe is still a point of discussion amongst family members, even if "the best yet" seems to be grandmother Jolanda's. On Saturdays, between 2pm and 4pm, while the bakery was closed, they would break 80 eggs and knead the dough by hand. They would swap places every 10 minutes to avoid arm cramps.

The bakery is now established, Rome is rich and Alessandro and Pierluigi work at the bakery despite the fact that they are still attending school and despite their adolescent restlessness. Rita keeps a watchful eye on the whole operation.

In the summer of 1992 a delicatessen on Via dei Giubbonari, not far from the bakery, closes. The plot lays empty for a few months until Marco decides to take it over in 1993 and extend the bakery's business. What was once compacted into a corner of the bakery explodes and expands. A grand counter with cold cuts and cheeses becomes a fully-fitted neighbourhood general store filled with detergents, boxed biscuits and brooms. The bakery adds a Delicatessen with general store to its business and divides it between bread, cakes, cold cuts and cheeses.

Twenty-four hours are no longer enough, says Marco.

In the place where the current Delicatessen kitchen stands, there was a blackened corner with a free-standing stove and a large "callaro", a copper pan used to cook the coppa di testa – boiled salami from humble cuts of pork. Above the extractor hood the Rosciolis would find a stone engraved with the head of a pig.

Luciana

Right at the beginning of the Salumeria Roscioli – Roscioli Delicatessen –, a young, shy girl came to help Marco with his new business. She was good at accounts, sweet, not a fan of crowds.

Luciana was born in Vicolo della Vaccarella, not far from Campo de' Fiori and entered into the Roscioli family's story quite silently. At school, in Corso Francia – where her mother worked –, she was ashamed to say that she lived in the "centre" because at that time the centre was still a run-down area of houses without heating with a reputation for unsavoury characters. Times would soon change and what she thought was a temporary job would soon become a job for life.

Luciana would be the centre of the new business' accounting and management and would provide balance to the entire place. Spaces were compacted and she adapted herself to the small corner, leaning against the window that she was given to manage the cash register.

She was tiny and squeezed her elegant body between the cash register counter and the boxes of wine. Immersed and almost camouflaged among the paperwork and produce on sale, over the years Luciana ended up doing everything that first Marco and then Alessandro were not able to do. She is another positive woman, an effective operator and an essential cog in the Roscioli machine.

In the beginning the Delicatessen had the same customers as the business that had previously occupied the site, yet it struggled to take off. The counter offered a standard range and the first supermarket in the area seemed threatening. Alessandro left the bakery and began working full time at the Delicatessen. It was 1993.

Having set his studies aside, Alessandro decided to study in another way and indiscriminately devoured everything he could get his hands on in terms of books on wine, cheese and cured meats.

Refined cheeses began to appear on the Delicatessen counter alongside the Galbanino: a cave-aged Emmental, a Castelmagno... However, these solitary "gems" got lost between anonymous Pecorino varieties, industrial Caciotta cheeses and packed cooked ham. The products on the counter would become the symbol of the transformation that would take almost 10 years to complete, a generational turnover that even today is still ripe with challenges and debate.

The metamorphosis did not only occur within the family, but was much further reaching. From the primitive collection at the beginning, now the desire for quality and not only quantity began to assert itself. It was here that the analysis of new customers came into play, those who were not always happy with the standard range. The product range grew, the exclusivity of which would soon go on to be called "niche".

OLIO

Pierluigi

Pierluigi was also born in Centocelle, in 1974. Like Alessandro, he studied for his diploma at the technical upper-secondary school in Testaccio. Before half eight in the morning he would make a few deliveries for the bakery in a green ape, a little, three-wheeled truck with "Roscioli" written on it, which he would then park in front of his school. In the afternoons, when he wasn't practicing karate – a lifelong passion – he would spend a few hours at the bakery.

Rita made sure he travelled from a young age. Pierluigi spent at least a month and a half every year travelling the world, learning English and visiting other cities. His first trip was to Eastbourne in the south of England when he was thirteen years old. It was in 1987 and that would only prove to be the start of a long series of work-study trips in the United Kingdom and the United States.

These trips would open up Pierluigi's mind, which would become filled with new ideas and inspiration for the future, for his family and, above all, for Alessandro.

Pierluigi returned from the Big Apple with the story of a stunning shop at 560 Broadway. Dean & DeLuca featured a counter for olives that was 4 metres long, simple, linear, all-metal fittings and a bewildering selection of gastronomic delights. While he recounted all this, he was aware that he was planting a seed for the delicatessen project that would soon come to fruition.

The format of gourmet food and wine displayed on designer shelves (in stark contrast to the industrially produced products displayed in standard supermarket aisles) began to take shape, inspired by that first Dean & DeLuca on Broadway and his trip, as was the idea to add a space to try these niche products in store. It was during this time that all the great concept stores worldwide were dedicating areas, indeed whole floors, to wine and food. The forerunners to Eataly in Italy came much earlier, dating back to that shop on Broadway, to the sixth floor of KaDeWe in Berlin, to La Fayette Gourmet in Paris and to the gourmands stands of Harrods in London.

Alessandro and Pierluigi decided to renovate the Delicatessen. The selection of cold cuts and cheeses had to be changed completely and the food had to be

Pier Luigi
Roscioli
G-SHOCK

SOLAIA
BAROLO
BAROLO
BAROLO
PECCHENINO
PECCHENINO
PECCHENINO
CONTERNO
MUSELLA
AMARONE
PIEROPAN
PIEROPAN
assolto

paired with a lovely selection of wines. The two brothers were innovators and daring, but they had to build a base of knowledge and know-how that only existed on paper at that point. Pierluigi suggested that Alessandro become a sommelier and that he should start studying the world of wine. He began to diligently frequent the bakery, learning about dough and baking from his father and the bakers.

The first project at the "New Delicatessen" involved reversing the structure of the counter by placing it on the window side, shortening it, removing the part that used to be reserved for bread and adding a few tables. There was no kitchen, nor chimney flue, so the idea was to just offer a few platters with cold cuts and cheeses and a glass of wine. It wasn't clear to either of them that shortly thereafter cooking with the products on the counter would be inevitable.

Fabio Del Frate, the owner of a renowned Roman wine bar, had been a supplier of Roscioli Delicatessen from the very beginning and it was he who would lead Alessandro not just towards the world of wine, but who would also introduce him to the network of wine producers and distributors in Rome. He was a godfather of elegance, Fabio, of good living, restaurants, boats, cashmere and intense days spent at the seaside together. Through Fabio, Alessandro would meet Cristiana Lauro, an extremely charming woman and a fine wine connoisseur. During the first few years of the New Delicatessen he would establish an important relationship with her, rich in experiences and discoveries.

16th December 2002

On the 29th June 2002 the Delicatessen closed for renovations. The work would last for over 5 months.

The renovated space was innovative. There were no rustic accents, no references to the past. Rather, it was a box-like space of rough brickwork with ironwork fittings to hold the countless jars of speciality products and bottles of wine that framed the range of cured meats and cheeses on the counter. Quite different from what Rome was used to.

A week after the New Delicatessen opened, Alessandro and Pierluigi decided to add the kitchen. They didn't have planning permission, they didn't have gas, they didn't even have a chef, but both knew that if they did not do it now, they would never be able to do it. The spot that held the copper pot was set up with a tiny kitchen, 10 square metres in total. An external chimney flue was built in one night. The scaffolding was assembled in a hurry, and covertly.

The next day Pierluigi bought white chef uniforms. Behind the counter he imagined an important, authoritative charcutier, one with a chef's jacket, not just your usual, run-of-the-mill deli worker. From then onwards Marco never ceased to make fun of the new charcutiers, calling them "four-barrel admirals".

The 16th December was set to be the day of the reopening, but unfortunately the counter of the delicatessen was empty. There were only five slabs of prosciutto, still in their packaging. Alessandro was up a ladder trying to arrange bottles of wine on the metal shelves. The decision was made not to open, given the fact that the couriers were running late and there was no merchandise to prepare the counter.

At 6pm "il Direttore" – Stefano Bonilli – passed by, as he did every day. Alessandro informed him about the postponement of the opening and il Direttore began a unique operation of persuasion that ended in a kind of occupation. Many curious onlookers had actually crowded around the entrance, attempting to get a look at the new Roscioli Delicatessen set up. After convincing Alessandro not to postpone the opening any further, il Direttore opened the door to the Delicatessen and let people in, quite without warning. It was to be an unexpected inauguration made of nothing more than prosciutto and bubbly.

€ 30,00 AL KG
CIPOLLINE BORETTANE
€ 40,00 AL KG
OLIVE TAGGIASCHE "RIVIERA DI PONENTE" DENOCCIOLATE
€ 42,00 AL KG

Il Direttore

Stefano Bonilli had known Alessandro and Pierluigi since they were children, since the time he had chosen Campo de' Fiori as his home. The story of this family (and this book) is a story he knew and cared about deeply, and whose development and progress he had followed over the years. With him, Pierluigi and Alessandro had grown up, first as the children of the baker downstairs, then as unsuspecting, anonymous deli owners, and lastly, as a brilliant new generation of bakers-cum-restaurateurs. It is clear that a lot of the advice, tips, invitations and criticism that he offered over the years presented new and productive avenues to explore for the Roscioli family and it is just as clear that the mark left by his passing is still deep and painful.

A passionate journalist, and founder of the Gambero Rosso food and wine magazine, il Direttore (the Editor), as everyone loved to call him, was a regular at Roscioli. Every day, whether stopping by for some shopping, a chat or a solitary lunch, he provided criticism and suggestions, and questioned and praised when there was the need to do so, even just by giving a look of pleased approval or a scowl of deep disdain. His restaurant guides and reviews served to help the Roscioli enterprise, even when it was only criticism, because it was direct and clear. His contacts extended the universe of the Salumeria and introduced it to a more international set.

Near to the counter, directly to the right of it, there is a table, table 14. Even though il Direttore is now no longer with us, that table will always be the table of il Direttore.

The first few months in the life of the Delicatessen were completely improvised. Filling the cheese and cured-meat counter completely took three months. The first waiters and kitchen staff moved in a direction that was very far from the idea of service and cooking that, slowly but surely, Alessandro was building in his head. The first menus offered tacos, trout and mushrooms, pappardelle pasta with red wine and ricotta, duck speck and langoustine with a dusting of coffee and lemon.

Creativity was present and accounted for, perhaps overly so, but there was no flavour. The counter products, the centre of the Delicatessen, were missing and, more importantly, Rome and its cuisine were missing too. For months new chefs and new staff came and went until finally they found the right balance: the circle had been squared and they were heading in the right direction.

Roscioli

Giusy

You need a woman with years of experience in the restaurant business to be able to offer a warm and professional welcome that is both personal and elegant, even at the tiny tables without tablecloths and in the small spaces of the Delicatessen.

The daughter of Antonietta – a strong, passionate Roman woman – and Gaetano – a Palermo-born chef – Giusy had long ago followed her father and her family's footsteps into the catering world, which her father had chosen as his trade, teaching himself as he went. Giusy worked as a waitress from the age of sixteen. She did so instinctively, following the few rules experience had taught her concerning manners, style and common sense. When she arrived at the Delicatessen having gone through a succession of difficulties outside of work, she was able to find a subjective, personal tone and to give the Roscioli Delicatessen an identity. Even her doubts about the menu on offer would encourage Alessandro to change direction in the kitchen. Giusy remembered a Tunisian chef that she and her father had worked with previously in a wine bar and she asked him to come work at the Delicatessen. The connection between Giusy and Nabil, the energy around the new project and the first insights of Alessandro concerning the route to take were the keys to change.

For Alessandro, the initial months and years were a period of exploration. He dove deep into Rome's restaurant scene, losing himself amongst the cheeses of the most beautiful shop in Rome – La Tradizione –, studying Casa Bleve and drawing inspiration from it, discussing the new wine list with Fabio at the Enoteca Del Frate and exploring traditional Roman dishes with his friend, chef Arcangelo Dandini.

These are the years in which he takes the train to go to San Vincenzo to explore the cooking recommended by il Direttore, the innovative, soulful menus of the legendary chef, Fulvio Pierangelini. After a lovely lunch featuring sharply defined flavours, after a neat succession of concise dishes with two, maximum three, ingredients on the plate, Fulvio invites the small group of Roman restaurateurs to come to the family business, where they produce impressive joints of cured Cinta breed pork, where they study nutrition in order to make special eggs, which are

almost savoury, where they produce excellent olive oil and where the wine cellar holds fabulous magnums. That lunch and that afternoon spent together marks a turning point for Alessandro. Flavour and simplicity are key.

At the top of the new menu, from then onwards, he would write a phrase by Fulvio Pierangelini: "The simpler the cooking appears to be, the more attentive you must be because the room for error increases". The lesson is clear: do not pursue complexity but simplicity, though this is not same as simple and straightforward, quite the opposite. Pure, clear flavour must be preserved in its essence and never disguised or confused.

In 2004, once again on the advice of il Direttore, Alessandro dined at El Bulli in Roses, Spain. He didn't understand what was going on during that strange dinner, although something was definitely happening. The research and innovation of genius chef Ferran Adrià got under his skin and a Carbonara in a consommé with gelatine tagliatelle offered a lingering symbol of absolute extremism for him to reflect on.

Nabil

Nabil is the Tunisian version of the *Evening Shadow*, the famously slender Etruscan statue from the town of Velathri, later Volterra. He is a sculpture by Alberto Giacometti made flesh and bone. His thinness makes him 2D, as if his body were missing the third dimension, as if it had come to be moulded to fit the meagre 10 square metres of the Roscioli kitchen. Upon leaving that microscopic space, it is as if Nabil has been hollowed to a line.

Nabil was born in 1964 in a small town 10 km from Monastir, on the Tunisian coast. He loved to travel and one summer holiday he arrived in Pantelleria. He would return often, whenever he could, to this island in the middle of the Mediterranean. He adored the scent of oregano, the breeze, the fish and the sea.

Nabil
Salumeria con Cucina
Roscioli

In 1987 he decided to stay on the island and found himself work, gardening during the day and washing dishes at night. He lived in Monastero, up high, at the centre of the island, and every day he would hitchhike to get home from the restaurant. Francesco Cammarata, an avid chef, and his wife ended up adopting him. In just a few weeks Nabil went from washing dishes to working increasingly in the kitchen. At the Tu e Basta, as the restaurant was called, Nabil began to understand the magic of what it was to be a chef, he got to know the ingredient that he had always adored – fish – and followed every gesture and technique attentively.

After a brief period in Palermo, Nabil decided to take the advice of this first teacher, who could see something special in him, a rare ability, an innate speed and elegance. This young Tunisian chef wanted to grow and gain experience that went beyond Sicily. He saw an ad in the paper: "For a new opening in the Parioli area, Roman entrepreneur seeks Sicilian chef". There are less than 100 km between Pantelleria and Tunisia and Nabil was more of a Sicilian than a Tunisian chef. Francesco Cammarata called the Roman entrepreneur and sang Nabil's praises. The interview and kitchen trial in a hotel on Via Po went extremely well: caponata, panelle fritters and stuffed sardines astounded the project's financier and Nabil remained in Rome. It was 1999. A year later his wife would join him in the capital.

At La Méditerranée restaurant in the Parioli area, a well-to-do Rome neighbourhood, Nabil was in charge of pasta dishes and other primi piatti. All the staff were French, which was also down to the fact that behind the project lay the consultancy of Paul Bocuse and his deputy Roger Jaloux, 1976's "Meilleur ouvrier de France" (Best Craftsman of France). For Nabil, Jaloux would prove to be the one who would teach him the basics, technique, rigour and rules. The nouvelle cuisine at La Méditerranée was elegant and minimal. The setting was entirely French yet the flavours were totally Italian, with the exception of the butter which entered Nabil's world soft and supple. It was an oily and versatile ingredient that Nabil would learn to understand and use skillfully.

Two years later the French staff left the project. The investing lawyer became the Italian consul in Jamaica and decided to close the restaurant.

Nabil was left with five folders full of recipes given to him by the French: basic preparations, stocks, fish, meat and patisserie.

After a brief interlude in Palermo, a place where his wife did not want to raise their children, Nabil went back to Rome. A few rather lacklustre experiences followed and then he began to work with a Sicilian chef at Bric. His connection with Sicily never seems to have left him. The chef at Bric was Gaetano, Giusy's father, and shortly afterwards Nabil would find his way to Via dei Giubbonari.

After a one-day trial in the kitchen, Nabil officially became a chef at the Salumeria Roscioli. He had never made a Carbonara in his life and he hardly recognised any of the products on the counter. Long days spent in the kitchen with Arcangelo Dandini – Alessandro's friend and an outstanding chef of rare finesse – would be required to teach him the basics and fundamentals of Roman cooking. Arcangelo could see a particular speed and turn of hand in Nabil, even though he knew nothing of Roman cuisine.

Although he does not eat pork for religious reasons, and despite being no great fan of dairy products and cheeses, over the years Nabil would hone his technique thanks to his extremely strong spirit of observation and total dedication. When you ask how he can never have tried a Carbonara, he answers, saying, "you need to speak to pasta, trying it is not important. I can recognise perfection from the colour and, more importantly, from the smell".

In the more than ten years he has been at Roscioli, Nabil has brought a unique, technical, intuitive and personal perspective to a Delicatessen that has, at last, found its own voice in the kitchen.

With the cooking up to speed, Roscioli began to establish itself in the first food and wine guides and in the press. The location of the Delicatessen helped, given that a good proportion of the press in the sector lived in the area. Bonilli, il Direttore, chose it as his dining hall. Giacomo A. Dente, the nickname of a refined foodie that wrote up his reviews every week in the "Messaggero" newspaper, was right at home here. Luigi Cremona lived above the bakery. Daniele Cernilli would go back and forth between Roscioli and Il Goccetto, another famous wine bar in the centre. The first article that was published in the "Messaggero" declared:

"It is a sign of great civilisation and evolution in taste to find that this old shop behind Campo de' Fiori, an off-shoot of the famous bakery nearby, has been able to become a refined spot for gourmets, all thanks to the passion of the latest generation of the family that owns it. Here you can buy wine and other products, as well as stay for a snack in the finest wine-bar style" (Lo spuntino di mezzanotte dietro Campo de' Fiori/ The midnight snack behind Campo de' Fiori, by Giacomo A. Dente).

Just a few days after it opened, without even realising it, the opening hours of the Delicatessen began to extend to midnight: you could eat at all times and everywhere, even standing or on the stairs.

On 27th September 2003 took place the first edition of Notte Bianca in Rome. Before the city, and the entire country with it, were hit by the biggest blackout in the history of the national electricity grid, Roscioli set its first record: despite only having 50 seats spread between two rooms, over 460 people would eat at the Delicatessen over the course of that long night and a further 500 would be turned away.

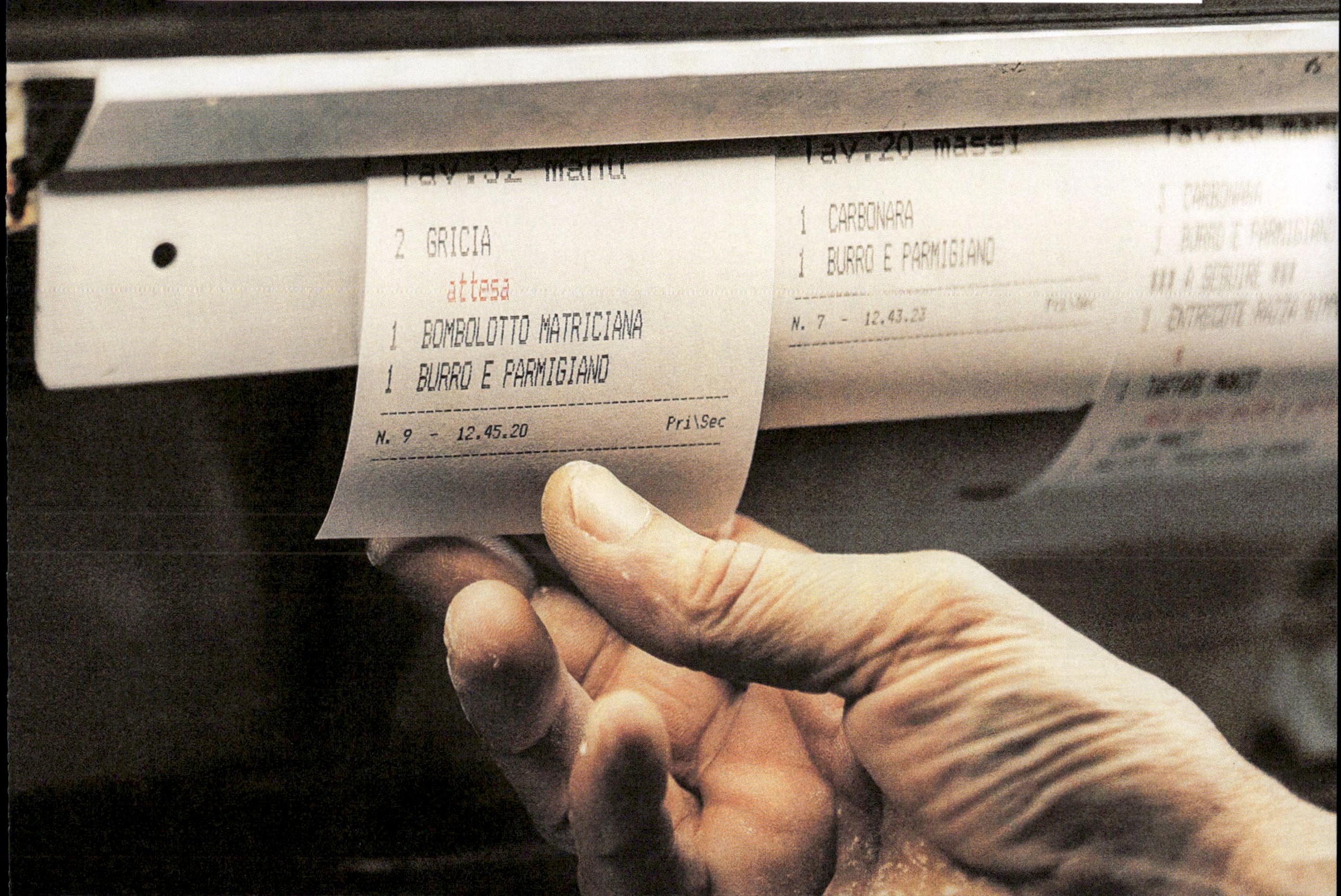

Success was gradual and steady. The counter filled with cheeses. Carlo and Giovanni Guffanti Fiori, great affineurs from Arona, on Lake Maggiore, would set aside rounds of wonderful Gorgonzola, a fine Castelmagno and intense alpine Fontina cheeses, together with a beautiful, rich selection of other Italian cheeses.

Over 100 French cheeses alternated vertically in terms of maturity with great and "noble" Italian cheeses, such as "Vacche Rosse" Parmigiano Reggiano, Pecorino Sardo from Gavoi, Asiago Stravecchio, and Monte Veronese and Piave made with milk from the high summer pastures. In addition to aged cheeses, fresh and semi-aged cheeses immediately began to take up space: soft cheeses from the Langhe region, Robiola varieties, an interesting selection of goat cheeses (some even produced using natural lactic coagulation or with vegetable "rennets") not to mention stracchino cheeses and mascarpone. One corner held stacks of what the menu described as "stinky cheeses" from all over the world: blue cheeses made with cow's, goat's or sheep's milk and enriched with precious natural moulds. These could be matched with honey and mostarde preserves.

Every day extremely fresh mozzarella would arrive from Paestum, as well as burrata cheese from Andria. A canopy of cured meats, caciocavallo and provola cheeses from southern Italy hung over the entire counter.

On rotation – when there was milk, when the curds came out just right, when the rennet made of fig leaves worked or the alpine pastures allowed for exceptional productions – small and extremely rare cheeses would arrive: Pecorino from Giuseppe Cugusi in Gavoi, goats cheese from Girgentana goats made by Giacomo Gatì in Campobello di Licata and the fantastic Robiola cheeses made by Valentina Canò of the La Via Lattea cheese company.

Massimo Spigaroli and Fulvietto Pierangelini selected coppa and culatelli cured meats at the perfect level of ageing. The prosciutto counter expanded month by month until there were six hand-cut hams and ten machine-sliced varieties on display. Smaller prosciutto varieties were added alongside San Daniele, Parma, Cormons, Sauris and the flavoursome prosciutto from the Monti Sibillini. They came from the small thighs of native, wild Italian pigs: Grigio del Casentino from Simone Fracassi, biodynamic, wild Cinta Senese and Nero Siciliano raised by the Agostino family in the Monti Nebrodi. The parterre of Spanish jamon offered rare

GUANCIALE ARTIGIANALE
DI BASSIANO
BASSO LAZIO

salumeria con cucina

and extremely well-aged gems. To these were added artisan *'nduja*, coriander-flavoured salami from Itri, Cresponetto salami from Varzi, sopressata salami from Gioi, near Salerno, and the soft ciausculo salami of the Marche region.

The search for producers also extended to fruit, vegetables, jams and preserves. The Agnoni family and their artichokes "alla cafona" would become the symbolic product of the store: preserved in oil, yet featuring the fresh flavour of artichokes marinated with local lesser calamint.

This partnership was not only a business agreement between entrepreneurs, but rather a relationship that would become familial, a friendship. Alessandro would develop a bond that went above and beyond a simple partnership or business relationship with the De Carlo family. Every entrée, every appetiser, every mozzarella dish at the Delicatessen was accompanied by a generous serving of the De Carlos' confit cherry tomatoes. Intense and flavoursome, they came preserved in Apulian extra-virgin olive oil made from the Bitritto and Conca Barese varieties.

Truffles came every week, sometimes even every day, brought by Dino Paolini, a dealer in white truffles (and other specialities), with whom the Delicatessen has collaborated for twenty years: the best of Langhe, Molise, Abruzzo tubers, as well as Umbrian and Siena varieties. There was also a selection of wild salmon, caviar, sensational Cantabrian anchovies and the more intense variety from Anzio, as well as tuna from Trapani or from Vulcano and lagoon-caught Mullet Bottarga from Cabras – the best of the best.

The shelves filled with artisan durum wheat pasta. The perfect dish was studied for each type of pasta and different producers were chosen according to different "vintages" and their development. The partnership with Abruzzo pasta makers, Verrigni, has been constant. Our twenty-year trade with the historic Apulian pasta makers, Benedetto Cavalieri, is such that the company decided to make 1 kg packs especially for restaurants, all thanks to Roscioli, which gets through copious amounts of Spaghettoni pasta every day.

Over time, the walls of the Delicatessen came to be covered by wheels of Parmigiano Reggiano, jars, tins, boxes, but wines especially. The bottles would multiply and grow year after year.

For the opening 500,000 euros were invested in products and ingredients, and half of that sum was spent in bottles of wine. In the beginning the wine list was predominately Italian, with a few interesting forays into French labels. Bottles were everywhere, there were even two store rooms behind the walls of the room on the lower floor. The racks would slowly but surely reach the rafters, the shelves would become stronger and more solid and the spaces were streamlined as much as possible. Over the years the deli's external wine cellars (in neighbouring basements and beneath the bakery) would increase to three and there would be more than 35,000 bottles.

When, one day, il Direttore walked into the Delicatessen and, stunned by the abundance and the quiet chaos on the shelves, said under his breath, "I thought I had walked into Cantarelli", Alessandro realised that their first milestone had been reached.

Maurizio

After finishing the lunch shift Maurizio takes a piece of paper and, as if it were a daily mantra, goes through all the cases at the Delicatessen, checking every shelf and every bottle. When he sees a space, he notes it down on the paper and continues on. The daily check of all the bottles on the shelves is almost like a roll call, he the meticulous teacher marking the register.

He arrived at Roscioli after a lifetime spent in wine and today has "the good luck to work with a dear friend, Alessandro, and to spend each day having fun with wine".

With his mane of dreadlocks, Maurizio Paparello moves like the shadow of a lion and looks over the narrow rooms full of customers. Then, when needed, he looks into the customer's eyes, communicating his full, magical attention. His approach is not classic, nor slick or rigid, but soft, playful, fun and entertaining, yet always authoritative and serious at the same time.

From Teodoro Bugari, a founding member of the Italian Sommelier Association, his first great teacher, he learnt that to be a "wine professional" you do not need to twirl the glass to see the "legs", it does not matter if you can recognise one of the 300 scents that a particular wine surely possesses and it's not important to be able to

ORNELLAIA
MONTEVERTINE
MONTEVERTINE

recognise a wine from its aroma and bouquet. What is important is knowing the wine and its producer, travelling, seeing the terroirs up close, smelling them and tasting them, thereby creating a truly personal approach. Most of all, you need to have fun.

Which is what he has always done. After working the last few summers of high school at the Il Castro restaurant in Morrovalle, sparking his passion for wine, Maurizio went on to travel and explore constantly: Spain, France – a lot of France – but Tuscany and Piedmont first and foremost. In 1994, together with the chef Michele Biagiola, he found his first opening in the restaurant trade: a family restaurant in Cummorano, in the Marche region, with thoughtfully prepared local dishes and a great passion for wines.

Their passion and cooking are such that in 1999 the Giosuè family asked Maurizio and Michele to take a leap forward and transform Le Case in Macerata, a stunning structure for events and banquets, into a gourmet restaurant. They were intense years, full of experimentation and fun. Accolades and a Michelin star would soon arrive.

In April 2005 Maurizio threw himself into a new adventure, a champagne bar offering hand-cut prosciutto in the centre of Rome. It was at the Vino Garage, a small Carbonari bar, that the Roscìolis would meet Maurizio, between bubbly and Pata Negra ham. As soon as the Vino Garage started to suffer and change direction, Maurizio decided to leave and began to work in Via dei Giubbonari. It was a brief interlude because, despite the fact that he liked his position, Maurizio accepted a job with Mario Panciroli in Milan. A pianist and great wine collector, Panciroli was another wine master with whom Maurizio would discover how to work with wine outside of a restaurant setting.

Great trips, impressive tasting sessions, lovely meetings with producers and a wealth of wine events on the Milan drinking scene would allow him to try great drinks and provide him with a significant experience base. When Maurizio decided to return to Rome in 2007 and go back to working with Roscioli, he was welcomed with open arms. The wine list at the Delicatessen was expanded, and many gaps filled in. A large number of French labels were added to the list with multiple vintages for the customer to choose from. Entire ranges were bought from wineries. They took part in auctions and bought directly from small producers, favouring direct contact with small companies.

In addition to these riches from the upper echelons of the world of wine – great labels, great vintages – Maurizio brought balance to the constant relationship between high and low: the value of humility in the hard work that exists behind the wine world and the work of the restaurant floor, the value of land and of people.

The best Carbonara in the world

It was 15th January 2008 and at the Città del Gusto culinary institute, a bastion of Gambero Rosso, Stefano Bonilli had organised a historic event: Carbonara Day.

When Rosario Scarpato and Mario Caramella from the Gruppo Virtuale Cuochi Italiani, an online community of Italian chefs abroad, announced that they were organising a day celebrating Italian cuisine worldwide and dedicating it to Carbonara, Bonilli decided to take part and became the promoter and spokesman for the Italian challenge. Carbonara has become the symbol of an evolving Italian cuisine, even if we exclude the extremes and the extremism of this evolution: cream, garlic, onion and the many other "extras" that are prohibited by tradition yet are widely used worldwide, even on the Michelin-starred tables of famous chefs such as Joël Robuchon in Paris, Mario Batali in New York or Piero Selvaggio in Los Angeles.

The Carbonara Day contest involved many participants, yet the nuances of perfection would be contested by two restaurants in Rome, the birthplace of Carbonara: L'Arcangelo and the Salumeria Roscioli.

Fulvio Pierangelini's Gragnano pasta dressed with guanciale and Arcangelo Dandini's Pecorino cheese from Rocca Priora – matured in house – and Madagascar pepper and organic eggs lost out – but only just – to Benedetto Cavalieri spaghettone dressed with melting cubes of Conero guanciale, Paolo Parisi eggs, Pecorino Romano and Moliterno Pecorino cheese (50% each), together with a blend of different kinds of pepper (Sichuan, Malaysian and Indian), the creation of chef Nabil Hadj Hassen of the Salumeria Roscioli. The news resonated internationally. Journalist Ian Fisher from the Herald Tribune reserved the front page for the curious story of a Tunisian chef who had become the *leading* proponent of the iconic Italian dish, and the whole world, from Denmark to Japan, was soon to pick up the story.

Chefs

It is autumn 2008 when the Les Grandes Tables du Monde association, the league that brings together the best chefs and restaurateurs worldwide, arranges an event for the best chefs the world over in Rome. They arrived in their masses to the capital, including Paul Bocuse, Georges Blanc, Marc Haeberlin and with them Livia and Alfonso Iaccarino, Annie Feolde and Giorgio Pinchiorri, Nadia and Antonio Santini, Gualtiero Marchesi, Massimo Bottura, Mauro Uliassi, Fulvio Pierangelini, Antonino Cannavacciuolo, the brothers Alajmo, Gennaro Esposito.

Before the gala dinner at the Hilton, the chefs met for lunch at Roscioli. Together with all the Italian food critics that were also present for the launch of the Gambero Rosso guide at Città del Gusto, it was a gastronomic outing of unusual prestige, filled with tastings and discussion.

Gualtiero Marchesi, after the first round of dishes at the Delicatessen and a textbook Carbonara, asks for the definitive test: a dish consisting simply of pasta, butter and parmigiano. Nabil improvises and the verdict is outstanding. Maestro Marchesi thinks the pasta is too al dente but finds the creamy emulsion of cheese and butter to be masterful. This provides Nabil with a great feeling of satisfaction.

Over the years the Salumeria would become a point of reference for many chefs.

For Salvatore Tassa, a leading, and inventive, proponent of the cooking of the Lazio cuisine, it is a model and continuous yardstick. Massimo Bottura is extremely enamoured with the place. The Roca brothers are regulars, and you could easily walk into the Delicatessen one day and find René Redzepi feeding his daughter tortellini in steaming broth. A sincere and mutual connection would be established with chefs around Rome. The brilliant Luciano Monosilio, once a student of Nabil and his second-in-command for a few years at the Delicatessen, considered Roscioli his second home. Enrico Pierri, owner of the San Lorenzo restaurant, just 100 metres from the Roscioli Bakery, becomes a neighbourhood friend, the sort that will stop by for a chat or to spend his breaks between one service and another. Marco Amato, director of the Imàgo restaurant at Hotel Hassler, is Alessandro's eternal opponent for games of tennis. Mario Sansone from the Marzapane restaurant and Alessandro Pipero from Pipero al

Rex are regular customers and companions on gastronomic explorations. Fulvio Pierangelini is Fulvio Pierangelini and as such, when he sits at the counter to drink a glass of bubbly accompanied by a Cantabrian anchovy, there is a hushed and magical atmosphere.

Trends and the gastronomic star system are overcome by the solid everyday machinations of constant quality, by the synchronised movements of the minuscule kitchen, by the quick and flexible service, by the suppliers that bring products in the morning and stop to have a coffee with the staff, by a covert bite of white pizza when a member of staff gets the munchies.

The staff team grows and evolves year after year. Alessandro is always behind the counter. If a glass needs cleaning or bread needs cutting, he does not shy away. In fact, after all is said and done, he prefers working behind the counter over everything else.

A regular customer comes to the counter every day, a Rome hotelier who has been following his daily ritual for over 10 years: eating lunch and dinner, in silence, two dishes at the counter. At Roscioli, the deli counter can switch from being a shared, social space, to become a place of unadulterated silence, isolation and respect.

Alessandro, brusque and often taciturn, communicates with his eyes and becomes animated with small gestures and details. Every so often his mobile vibrates and he moves away, leaving room for the staff. It is often for work, but sometimes, at least three times a week, it is his friend Vito Cinque, the manager of the Hotel San Pietro in Positano. A parallel destiny ties Alessandro to Vito: both run a family business alongside a brother – Pierluigi for Alessandro and Carlo for Vito. The two brothers are different. In some respects, they are even opposites, and their similarities are often odd and sources of humour. Often the relationship between Alessandro and Vito turns into playful complaints about the "wrongdoings" of their relative brothers, which is just pure, entertaining venting. From behind the counter at the Delicatessen Alessandro will send an insulting message to Vito and he, from behind the reception desk in the tiled foyer at his hotel, responds ironically with a "miserly" response. In order to stand behind a counter for 365 days a year and run demanding businesses that are increasingly complex to manage you need to have a few healthy outlets.

It is from behind that very counter that, in October 2006, Alessandro would meet Chiara, a brilliant and strong woman with whom he would build his family, with whom he would decide to get his body under control and deal with his weight problems, and with whom he would be able to unplug every day, even just for a minute, from the never ending work at the Delicatessen.

The private tasting room

Recounting the story of Roscioli and finding a place in which to explore it calmly with more time and space would become a real need over the years. In addition to Maurizio Paparello, a number of figures from the wine industry would come, go, arrive, set off again and stay. Gaetano Saccoccio, a wine philosopher, organised tastings and workshops and Valerio Capriotti would leave a Michelin star setting to return to Roscioli to offer his distinctive, elegant touch.

SCRAMBLER
DUCATI

It was in 2011 that the Rimessa Roscioli, a private tasting room, would be created in an annex of the Delicatessen, above one of the wine-filled cellars. Cooking spaghetti alla Carbonara and selling wine was no longer enough. A small and well-organised space, it was open only when customers would request it and, therefore, did not entail any waste while it only required a small number of waiting staff. Here, wine could be accompanied by cooking and charcuterie samples and tasting sessions, food and wine courses, lessons, workshops and seminars could be booked.

Alessandro Pepe would be the man to create it together with Alessandro and Maurizio, as well as run it day by day. Alessandro loved the world of wine, but had no interest in the restaurant floor. He is a nervous and restless man who, over ten years with Roscioli, has been able to implement a different and intelligent way of selling wine, of recounting it and of embarking on food and wine storytelling.

The private tasting room holds a lot of Alessandro – who is known as the Meneghino after the traditional Italian character in Commedia dell'arte theatre – and his Kafkaesque life that has seen everything happen. A little of his essence as a film director, documentarian, glass recycler on the streets of Dublin, novelist, waiter, taster, porter at the Mercati Generali marketplace, sales representative and cloakroom attendant can be found in the Rimessa.

From Marco Roscioli's bakery to the explosive success of the deli-restaurant, a lot has been achieved. The Roscioli format has been studied as a successful example in the Master of Management in Food & Beverage degree course at Milan's Bocconi University and within the Sole 24 Ore Food & Wine course on marketing and communication strategies. Over the years many entrepreneurs have asked to replicate the format in the United States, United Kingdom, Hong Kong, Singapore and Tokyo, without an agreement ever being reached. "The Delicatessen with kitchen cannot be replicated. It only works – if it works – this way. We are shopkeepers, we don't delegate," states Alessandro Roscioli. And when asked if their goals have been reached, he says that there are no goals.

INGREDIENTS FOR 4 PEOPLE

- 360 g Benedetto Cavalieri Spaghettoni (extra-long, extra-thick spaghetti)
- 240 g guanciale (cured pork cheek)
- 1 whole egg + 3 egg yolks
- 210 g Pecorino Romano
- 40 g "Vacche Rosse" Parmigiano Reggiano (aged 24 months)
- coarse salt
- 20 g freshly ground black pepper

CARBONARA

Carefully trim the guanciale, removing all the pepper and rind. Cut it into strips about 1 cm wide and then into 1 cm cubes. Brown them in a pre-heated frying pan on a high heat. Do not stir. Wait until the fat has begun to melt and one side is crispy and golden. Now stir and wait for all the fat to dissolve. Reduce the heat and leave the cubes of guanciale to caramelise for at least 20 minutes, then put them in a pan close by or over the oven so they will stay crispy. Finely grate the two cheeses with a traditional Italian-style grater (not the kind that grates into slices or curls) and mix them together. While the spaghettoni are cooking in salted water (which will take about 12-13 minutes), whisk the eggs in a plastic bowl – plastic is better as it doesn't heat easily. Add a handful of grated cheese and the freshly ground pepper and mix. If you can, use a mortar rather than a grinder so that the pepper is not too fine. When the pasta is almost done, drain it, making sure to keep a few ladles of the water. Put the pasta directly in the bowl with the eggs, pepper and cheese. Let it sit near to the stove or another heat source for about a minute, then add the crisped guanciale and spoonful of its fat. If you can, without using tongs or another implement, move the bowl in circles and up down to emulsify the eggs, cheese, and guanciale with the pasta. Work quickly, possibly helping it along by adding a little of the pasta water. The magic of a successful Carbonara all lies in this challenging moment of emulsifying the eggs, cheese and guanciale fat with the pasta water and the gluten of the pasta itself. Put a ball of pasta in the centre of each plate and season with extra cheese and pepper.

INGREDIENTS FOR 4 PEOPLE

- 280 g tonnarelli (spaghetti alla chitarra or square spaghetti)
- 400 g Pecorino Romano
- 130 g "Vacche Rosse" Parmigiano Reggiano (aged 24 months)
- 500 ml natural mineral water
- 30 g freshly ground black pepper *
- coarse salt

CACIO E PEPE/CHEESE AND PEPPER

Grate the two cheeses with a traditional Italian-style grater. Pour the cheese into a large bowl, mix gently and add 500 ml of lukewarm water. Blend with a hand blender until the mixture is smooth, silky, and somewhat dense: this is the perfect base for *cacio e pepe* or *pasta alla gricia.* Keep in mind that you can prepare this in a large batch and refrigerate it, well sealed, for up to a month. Cook the tonnarelli pasta in salted water and, in the meantime, take one big spoonful of the cheese base per person and place it in a pan without oil or water. As soon as the tonnarelli pasta is *al dente,* drain and pour it directly into the pan with the cheese base so that some of the cooking water emulsifies with the base, creating a creamy sauce. Put the pan on the stove and stir gently until the mixture formed from the cheese sauce, pepper, pasta water, and pasta gluten is sticky. To test, squeeze a drop between your thumb and finger and if the sauce is dense and forms strings, like glue, it's ready. Serve by placing a nest of tonnarelli pasta in the middle of a pasta dish, adding a spoonful of sauce and a sprinkle of cheese and pepper.

* PEPPER

With a cuisine such as that of Rome, which is based on a small number of strong flavours, the choice of pepper is essential. We decided to create our own, personalised aromatic mix with different kinds of pepper, as a sort of signature for those dishes where this spice is the star. After a quick toasting in the pan, crush equal parts Java pepper and Black Sarawak pepper in a mortar. Do not grind too finely or too far in advance – ideally, it should be ground immediately before use. Neither type of pepper is especially spicy and both have interesting aromatic profiles. The result is a pungent, resinous taste, with fresh balsamic notes reminiscent of juniper and myrtle.

INGREDIENTS FOR 4 PEOPLE

- 320 g mezze maniche pasta
- 280 g guanciale with its fat (cured pork cheek)
- 250 g Pecorino Romano
- 50 g "Vacche Rosse" Parmigiano Reggiano (aged 24 months)
- 180 ml natural mineral water
- 30 g freshly ground black pepper
- coarse salt

GRICIA

Take the guanciale and trim off any pepper, the rind, and any fat that is not opaque white. Cut it into 1 cm strips and then into 1 cm cubes. Put them in a frying pan and let them brown well. Without stirring, leave the cubes of guanciale until the fat renders and the first side is well toasted and golden, then flip them with a wooden spoon and let them cook in their fat for at least 20 minutes. Finely grate the two cheeses with a traditional Italian-style grater and mix them together. Put the cheese and lukewarm water together in a large bowl.
Mix with a hand blender until the mixture becomes smooth, silky and somewhat dense.
While the pasta is cooking in salted water, pour one large spoonful of cheese sauce per person into a saucepan (without oil or water). As soon as the pasta is *al dente*, drain it directly into the pan with plenty of the pasta water.
Add one spoonful of browned guanciale per person, one spoonful of fat, and 2 handfuls of grated cheese (for four people) and emulsify by stirring together for a minute or two.
Put the pan onto the heat and stir until the creamy mixture produced by the cheese sauce, pepper, cooking water, guanciale, and pasta gluten is sticky. Serve in a pasta dish, adding a ladle of sauce and a sprinkling of cheese and pepper.

INGREDIENTS FOR 4 PEOPLE

FOR THE TOMATO SAUCE

- 500 g peeled tomatoes
- 2 shallots
- 80 ml extra-virgin olive oil
- fine salt
- 320 g mezzi rigatoni pasta
- 280 g guanciale (cured pork cheek)
- 150 g Pecorino Romano
- 50 g "Vacche Rosse" Parmigiano Reggiano (aged 24 months)
- coarse salt

AMATRICIANA

Put all the raw ingredients for the tomato sauce into a saucepan: peeled tomatoes, salt, oil, and shallots. Let them cook for 20 minutes, then purée with a hand blender. Simmer on a low heat for another 15 minutes. Take the guanciale and trim off any pepper, rind, and any of the fat that is not opaque. Cut the guanciale into 1 cm strips and then into 1 cm cubes. Put the cubes of guanciale in a pan and brown them well, without stirring. When one side is crispy and golden, turn them over and let the guanciale cook in its fat for at least 20 minutes.
While the mezzi rigatoni pasta is boiling in salted water, finely grate the two cheeses and combine them. Drain the pasta once it is *al dente* and put it directly into a pan with two ladles of tomato sauce. Then add one spoonful of crispy guanciale per person and a small ladleful of fat from the guanciale.
Stir vigorously in the pan and add two handfuls of grated cheese. Serve in a pasta dish with a final sprinkle of Pecorino on top.

INGREDIENTS FOR 4 PEOPLE

420 g tortellini

FOR THE BROTH

2.5 l natural mineral water

1/2 Bresse chicken

1 head of celery

2 carrots

1 onion

1 whole clove

20 g peppercorns

TORTELLINI IN BRODO/TORTELLINI IN BROTH

The secret to this recipe is definitely the quality of the tortellini. Those served at the Salumeria come weekly from Bologna. They're small tortellini as dictated by Emilian tradition, made with a thin, delicate pasta and filled with prosciutto, Parmesan and a bit of mortadella. To make the broth, after passing the chicken over a flame to remove any remaining feathers, put all the ingredients in a big, roomy pot. Let it simmer for an hour and a half, then strain the broth through a linen cloth. Once it has cooled, remove the excess fat that has appeared on the surface and bring the broth to the boil. Pour in the tortellini and cook for 8 minutes. Serve hot!

INGREDIENTS FOR 4 PEOPLE

360 g Benedetto Cavalieri Spaghettoni (extra-long, extra-thick spaghetti)

240 g French sweet butter

220 g Anzio anchovies

coarse salt

"BURO" E ALICI/BUTTER AND ANCHOVIES

A seemingly simple pasta dish that hides a profound complexity: a harmonious union occurs between the pungency of the Lazio anchovies and the milky taste of great French butter. As the spaghetti is boiling in plenty of salted water, melt the butter in a pan, then add the anchovies. Stir until they dissolve. Drain the pasta and stir vigorously with the butter and anchovy mixture. Serve topped with a whole anchovy.

INGREDIENTS FOR 4 PEOPLE

- 360 g spaghetti alla chitarra
- 200 g Bluefin tuna from the island of Vulcano
- 100 g tuna *buzzonaglia* (dark meat from around the spine)
- 50 g *capuliato* (a thick paste of sun-dried, Sicilian tomatoes)
- 50 g pitted Taggiasca olives
- 5 g Salina capers
- 20 ml extra-virgin olive oil
- 1 clove of garlic
- 3 g dried chili pepper

SPAGHETTO TONNO E BUZZONAGLIA
TUNA BUZZONAGLIA SPAGHETTI

Desalt the capers by leaving them in water for at least one hour; remember to change the water a few times. Dice the olives finely to make a coarse paste. As the spaghetti boils in salted water, brown the garlic in a pan with a little oil, together with the chili pepper and wild fennel (pre-blanched in salted water). Remove the garlic, add the olives, the *capuliato* and half a ladle of hot water. When the pasta is 2/3 done cooking, add it directly to the pan with some of the pasta water, then add the capers, tuna and *buzzonaglia*. Stir gently and thicken the sauce by sautéing until the dish is cooked and has the proper consistency.

INGREDIENTS FOR 4 PEOPLE

- 480 g Spalla di San Secondo (in 4 slices) – traditional cured pork shoulder from San Secondo, near Parma
- 400 g buffalo mozzarella
- 4 slices of pan brioche al prosciutto (brioche with ham) *
- 60 g basil
- 120 g cherry tomato confit
- 10 g salt
- 15 g black pepper
- 120 g red wine jelly *
- 200 ml extra-virgin olive oil
- 3 ice cubes

HAMBURGER DI BUFALA
BUFFALO HAMBURGER

Using a hand blender, blend up the rinsed, de-stemmed basil, the extra-virgin olive oil and the ice cubes. Have the Spalla di San Secondo cut into slices about 3-4 mm thick. Cut the mozzarella into slices of at least 1 cm. Heat a grill and cook the slices of Spalla as if it were steak, but don't let it dry out. Meanwhile, toast a slice of brioche. When the Spalla is fully grilled, put it onto a cutting board and split it into three parts. Assemble the dish: top the toasted bread with wine jelly, a slice of mozzarella and a piece of Spalla, and repeat until you've used all the ingredients.
You'll get a tower of about three layers of Spalla and mozzarella. Finish each burger with a generous spoonful of cherry tomatoes and the basil sauce.

* RED WINE JELLY

- 2 l dry red wine
- 400 g sugar
- 4 sheets of isinglass (gelatine)

Soak the isinglass in cold water to soften. Dissolve the sugar in the wine and put on the stove. As soon as it's warm, wring out the softened isinglass and add it to the pan, leaving it to simmer for at least 10 minutes, until the spoon you're using to stir the mixture has a film of isinglass on it. This is the moment to seal the jelly in a jar if you want to keep it or put it in a container to cool if you are planning to use it right away.

* PAN BRIOCHE AL PROSCIUTTO
BRIOCHE WITH HAM

FOR THE BIGA

- 1 kg soft white flour (Italian 00 flour)
- 550 ml water
- 1 g fresh brewer's yeast

- 1 kg of biga
- 100 g soft white flour (Italian 00 flour)
- 600 ml water
- 20 g honey
- 20 g salt
- 100 ml extra-virgin olive oil
- 10 g brewer's yeast
- 300 g sweet prosciutto crudo trimmings
- 40 g Parmigiano Reggiano
- butter + flour for the moulds
- 1 egg + 50 ml whole milk for brushing

Mix the ingredients for the biga on a low speed for 10 minutes. Cover the ball of dough with a linen towel and let it stand at room temperature for 12-14 hours. When the biga has doubled in size, start kneading with the mixer, first on a low speed, for four minutes, then slightly higher for six minutes. Add the flour and water and knead vigorously until you get a smooth, elastic dough. Add the remainder of the ingredients. Split the dough into small loaves. Butter and flour two moulds and put one loaf in each. Brush lightly with beaten egg and milk and leave them to rise at room temperature for a couple of hours.
Bake at 220 °C for 35 minutes.

INGREDIENTS FOR 4 PEOPLE

- 1 kg pre-soaked salted black cod
- 200 g wild salad leaves (lamb's lettuce, rocket, baby lettuce)
- 15 ml extra-virgin olive oil
- 5 ml argan oil
- salt flakes
- 1 green apple
- 1/2 lemon

BACCALÀ "CARBONAIO"
BLACK COD "CARBONAIO"

Choose fillets of fish that are at least two fingers thick. On a well-heated griddle place the fillets skin-side down and let them cook for at least 7-8 minutes. The skin should be crispy, almost bubbly. Move the fillets from the griddle to an oven dish and bake for 5 minutes so that they are evenly cooked through to the centre. In a bowl, dress the salad with olive oil, a few drops of argan oil, and salt. Cut the green apple into thin slices, drizzle them with water and lemon juice and add them to the salad. Serve each piece of fish with a few flakes of salt on top and the salad on the side.

INGREDIENTS FOR 4 PEOPLE

- 12 Lazio lamb chops

FOR BREADING AND FRYING

- 200 g breadcrumbs (from the crust of Lariano bread)
- 200 g soft white flour (Italian 00 flour)
- 4 eggs + 2 yolks
- natural mineral water
- peanut oil

FOR THE CHICORY

- 1 bunch of wild chicory (about 600 g)
- coarse salt
- 40 ml extra-virgin olive oil
- 1 clove of garlic
- 1 chilli pepper
- salt flakes

COSTOLETTE DI AGNELLO E CICORIA
LAMB CHOPS WITH CHICORY

Coarsely grate the crust of a loaf of Lariano bread, preferably not a fresh one. Lightly pound the lamb chops with a meat mallet. Make a light batter with the flour, eggs, yolks, and half a glass of cold water. First dip the chops in the batter and then in the breadcrumbs, pressing firmly. Fry them in hot oil for 10 minutes. Wash the chicory thoroughly and blanch in a generous amount of boiling, salted water. As soon as the middle starts to soften, remove the chicory from the water. In a skillet, leave the oil to take on some flavour with the crushed garlic and a sliced chilli pepper. Once the oil is hot and the garlic has started to brown, remove the garlic and pepper and add the chicory. Sauté for 5 minutes and serve with the crisped chop, which should first be patted with kitchen paper to remove the excess fat. Before serving, add salt flakes.

INGREDIENTS FOR 4 PEOPLE

- 1 kg minced Piedmont beef, ideally from the thigh
- 500 g ground pork
- 500 g ground veal
- 200 g Bolognese mortadella
- 280 g "Vacche Rosse" Parmigiano Reggiano (aged 24 months)
- 4 g nutmeg
- zest of half a lemon
- half a clove of garlic
- 2 eggs + 1 yolk
- 3 slices of white bread → *recipe on page 242*
- 400 ml whole milk
- SALT AND PEPPER

FOR THE TOMATO SAUCE

- 1 kg peeled tomatoes
- 4 shallots
- 100 ml extra-virgin olive oil
- salt
- 400 g cooked polenta to accompany

POLPETTE DELLA TRADIZIONE ROMANA
TRADITIONAL ROMAN MEATBALLS

Grate the lemon zest making sure to only grate the yellow part. On a cutting board remove the crusts from the sliced bread and discard them. Leave the bread to soak in the milk. If you have your own mincer, grind the different meats yourself along with the mortadella and garlic. The result will be altogether better: smoother and more even. If you don't, start with quality minced meat and use a mezzaluna to cut the mortadella as finely as possible. Put all the meat, the mortadella, the soaked bread (after wringing out the excess milk), the cheese, and the finely chopped garlic in a very large bowl. Mix vigorously with your hands, until you have an even consistency, then add the salt, pepper, nutmeg, and lightly beaten eggs. Keep working until you get an even, pink mixture. Prepare the sauce by combining all the raw ingredients: peeled tomatoes, salt, oil, and shallots. Cook for 20 minutes, then purée with a hand blender. Leave the sauce to simmer on a low heat for another 15 minutes. Meanwhile, with wet hands, form the meatball mixture into small balls, rolling them gently – aim for about 70 g each. The water will seal the meatballs so there is no need to add flour or anything else. Once all the meatballs have been formed, dunk them into the boiling sauce and cook over a low flame for at least 45 minutes. Then take the polenta, cut it into thick slices at least 1 cm thick and grill them. Serve the meatballs hot, accompanied by the tomato sauce, grilled polenta, and a sprinkling of Parmesan.

INGREDIENTS FOR 4 PEOPLE

220 g mascarpone	3 egg yolks
110 g fresh cream	16 sponge fingers
120 g sugar	4 espressos
1 tablespoon natural mineral water	100 g unsweetened cocoa powder

TIRAMISÙ

With a stovetop espresso maker, make 4 espressos and leave them to cool. Whip the cream in a planetary mixer, cover with cling film and put in the refrigerator. Now put the egg yolks into the mixer and mix at a low speed for one minute. In a saucepan, dissolve the sugar in a spoonful of water. When the sugar has reached 116 °C, turn on the mixer and pour the hot syrup over the yolks and whip at full speed. Continue whipping until the mixture is cold. Turn off the mixer and stir in the mascarpone gently by hand. Take the whipped cream from the refrigerator and add it to the mixture, stirring from bottom to top. Soak the sponge fingers in the cold espresso, taking care not to break them. The biscuits should not absorb too much coffee – they should still be crunchy. Then take a small bowl, place two soaked sponge fingers, cover them with the mascarpone cream, add two more sponge fingers and cover with more cream. Sprinkle with cocoa powder before serving.

THE NEW BAKERY

Rethinking bread, researching new flour varieties and new ingredients: the way forward lies in the details.

THE OLD AND THE NEW

Every dough has been improved, the ingredients refined, the team grows, deliveries increase exponentially and the bakery becomes a workshop for constant research.

It's midnight and the bakery opens in the darkness of Via dei Chiavari. Renato, Scialbi and Lorenzo enter through the door next to the bakery's main entrance and start their shift.

They are the night bakers. They start kneading the dough for the Lariano bread, which takes more time, then the white rustic-style bread, the Tozzetti biscotti, using the same dough as the Lariano bread, and the first pizza dough. Every dough requires different ingredients, times and techniques. The flour – white for the most part – fills and then empties from the storeroom twice a week, in a continuous cycle. The dough for special breads are started around 1 in the morning: kamut, spelt, five grain, Ferrarese sourdough and corn bread. When the clock strikes 3 it is time for the second dough for the pizza, Lariano and rustic-style bread and the dough for rolls. It is all arranged according to a rhythm that does not follow a watch but rather a work cycle that is repeated 365 days a year.

The first round of bread has to be ready between 3 and 3.30 am, as it has to cool and deliveries need to get under way. The person that delivers bread in Rome is known as the "cascherino", the little helmet, as once upon a time deliveries were made on bike. The delivery guys, Roger and Davide, get to Roscioli at 5 in the

Casillo
GROUP
MOLINO
MAIONCHI
LUCCA

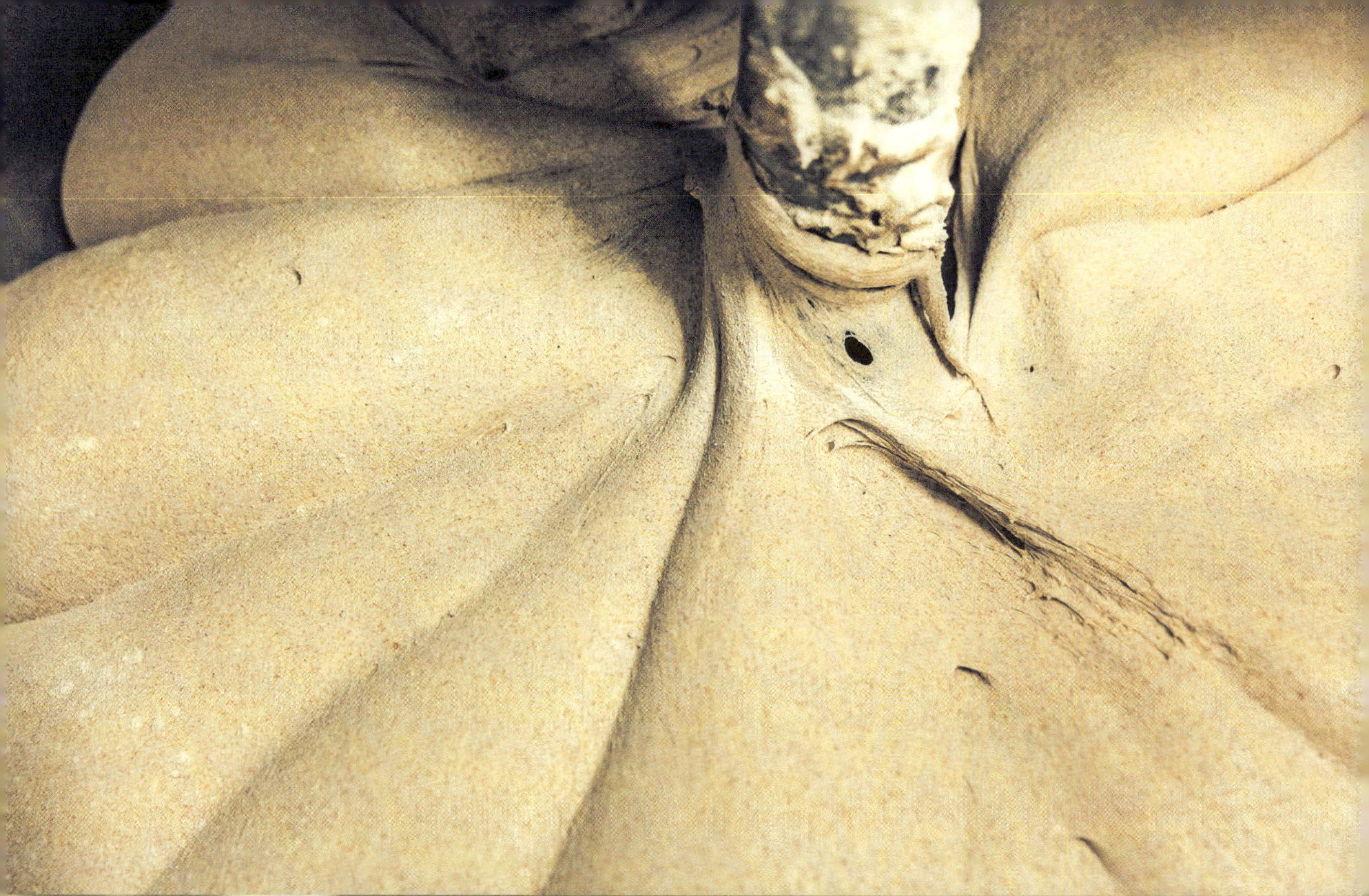

morning and prepare the 10 bags with bread for the first delivery to hotels, cafés and delis. They load up the Forno Roscioli-branded van and leave on the first delivery run. Each rough-paper bag has a small piece of paper attached, or the destination is written right on top. There are more than 130 clients spread all over Rome that are supplied daily, some even three times a day. Large hotels and boutique guesthouses that serve breakfast from 7 in the morning get their delivery in good time. Then it is the turn of the delis and restaurants.

Meanwhile, the pastry chefs, Paolo and Fabio, arrive around 5 and start to make the pastries for the shop: they turn on the oven and make the shortcrust pastry. The patisserie area is wedged between a large, upright rotary oven, a puff pastry machine and a kitchenette with stovetop, sinks and a worktop. Just outside you find the refrigerated rooms and fridges. The space to reduce and get ahead on work is not there. Every day the patisserie department makes everything that is needed to fill the counter, without pause. Ring cakes, tarts, biscotti and leavened goods are made from scratch every day. On rotation they make brutti ma buoni biscuits, wholegrain biscotti, sweet wine pretzels and rusks.

At 6.30 am Andrei starts to make pizza. At 7 the kitchen chefs, Fabrizio and Giorgio, begin work preparing that day's menu for the deli counter: they wash the chicory and when in season they prepare the artichokes, aubergine parmigiana, chicken and porchetta.

The first shop customers arrive at 8 and from that moment onwards, until 8 in the evening, it is a steady coming and going of people buying bread, a pastry, white pizza, red pizza, rice balls, people having breakfast, lunch or customers

devouring street food, leaning on one of the two cycle-mounted delivery boxes that sit outside the bakery. Between midday and 3 pm, when the influx of Romans and tourists transforms into a crowd, a queue forms in front of the bakery and a wholesale *déjeuner sur la rue* takes place.

In recent years Pierluigi has increasingly taken over the reins at the bakery. Respect for the work done by Marco and the family and the desire for innovation exist side by side, the border ever shifting in the direction of change. The initial signs of this desire for innovation could be seen ten years ago, when Pierluigi started to change the flour, no longer using the industrial Roman mill that supplied all of Rome, and started to search for small artisan producers or larger mills with which he could collaborate, to make customised flour blends for the individual bread types in the bakery.

The first "revolution" that marked the beginning of the new bakery dates bake to more than sixteen years ago when Pierluigi, through Francesco Roscino, tried an incredible salt that was quite unlike the salt usually implemented in bread dough.

Francesco is an old friend. He possesses a statuesque body and is athletic and sporty and for a long period he worked as a body guard to stars, models, singers and entrepreneurs. They were years spent on yachts, travelling, jet setting around and living the good life. During that time Francesco tried many foods that can be considered emblematic of luxury and splendour and would return from his work trips loaded with foie gras, butter and champagne. One year he returned from France with a strange and intense raw, grey salt.

Pierluigi tasted it and tried it in a Lariano bread dough, thereby discovering how living salt can make all the difference in a dough with live sourdough starter.

Without telling his father, Pierluigi ordered 100 kilos of raw salt from Normandy. After about a week, it was promptly delivered to Via dei Chiavari. The invoice arrived by mail before the merchandise, which greatly troubled Marco. It came from a company in the North of France. It was for 1,600,000 lire of salt which, according to his calculations, would soon be taking up the entire space of the bakery and its storerooms.

forno
il nostro pane e la nostra pizza (non
focaccia) sono prodotti seguendo il
processo di lievitazione naturale,
con lievito madre o con pasta acida
a pasta acida e
di Sorrento,
di segale e
kamut e

For Marco Roscioli, salt should cost 20, maximum 25 lire per kg, so he expected that 64 metric tonnes of salt would soon be delivered to the bakery. The argument that occurred between the two when Marco discovered that Pierluigi had brought a salt that "cost more than prosciutto" was epic and was the beginning of radical change that is still under way today.

This "salt revolution" would be followed by one concerning butter (which in certain doughs would come to replace the margarine), one involving the use of carefully-dosed, natural flavourings and the use of outrageous, lengthy leavening processes for sweet, leavened cakes like colomba, pandoro and panettone.

The desire to experiment and conduct research came to accompany the logic of pure financial reward, the philosophy of "primitive accumulation", the mechanical quality of a repetitive business that had gone forward for generations without its changing and solidity and tradition without modernisation.

Pierluigi, careful not to overdo it and without causing any damage, began to experiment, to see if he could take things even further. He concentrated heavily on iconic bread products, on Lariano bread, on pizza. In the summer of 2015 his classic panettone with candied orange and citron won the award for the best panettone tasted at the "Re Panettone" event in Milan, coming before historic names in the Italian pastry world. This was extremely satisfying, especially when you think about how this milestone was achieved, about how difficult it is to make great pastries in large quantities without prover retarders, temperature controlled rooms and large ovens. For Christmas 2015 panettone production migrated between the ovens at the Antico Forno Roscioli and the ovens in the new Roscioli bakery. In fact, in the summer of 2015 the Forno Roscioli bought a historic Roman patisserie just a short walk from the delicatessen and it was here that Pierluigi finally built a larger pastry workshop. Pierluigi and Francesco, the son of Giusy (who also happens to be the mother of Pierluigi's two children), moved, along with the parallel metal fixings used to hold the panettone upside down, from the bakery to Piazza Benedetto Cairoli, 16.

In January 2016, after having worked for almost fifteen years at the delicatessen, and after having (between a million other things!) married Pierluigi, Giusy decided she would join her husband in running the Antico Forno Roscioli. Something new was entering the world of this gourmet triangle in the heart of Rome.

INGREDIENTS

- 3.5 kg pork belly
- 1.5 kg pork loin
- 150 g natural salt
- 40 g rosemary
- 20 g fennel flowers
- 25 g fennel seeds
- 20 g black pepper
- 10 g ground chilli pepper
- 300 g spleen
- 300 g liver

PORCHETTA

Ask your butcher to give you a single cut from the side of the pig with the loin still attached to the belly and all the bones already removed, if possible. The important thing is that the skin is still securely attached to the meat and that, after trimming where required, you are left with a rectangle of meat at least 40 cm long. Lay out the pork, loin included, on a flat surface – marble is best – sprinkle on the salt and rub it thoroughly into the meat. Use a little water and keep massaging for another few minutes. Then add the chopped rosemary, fennel flowers, fennel seeds, the chilli pepper and the black pepper. If you fancy a taste of really authentic, traditional porchetta (the way the ancient Romans would eat their pork), you can even add a few pieces of liver and spleen. Roll the belly up tightly and, using a needle and twine, secure it with a stitch every 4-5 cm along the long edges and at the ends. Leave the raw porchetta to rest for at least 6 hours.
Before "tying" the porchetta, prick it with a sharp knife at various points along its length. Using an extremely long piece of twine, begin tying up the porchetta. This is an ancient and difficult art that uses the twine to hold the skin and meat tightly together. Start by tying the joint tightly lengthways with two, long loops, crossing the twine at the ends, then circle the rolled joint using a couple of loops of twine each time. Once the whole porchetta is properly tied up, place it in a large roasting tray and put it in the oven. The porchetta should be cooked "a mestiere", in other words over a long period of time at not too high a temperature. Start at 90-100 °C for an hour then gradually increase the temperature to 180 °C over the following 5 hours or so.
To make a classic porchetta sandwich all you need is two slices of Lariano bread and nothing else: all the seasoning and flavours are in the porchetta itself.

INGREDIENTS FOR 8 PIECES OF MOZZARELLA IN CARROZZA

- 4 large slices of white bread
  → *recipe on page 242*
- 1 mozzarella (250 g)
- 4 anchovies
- 2 slices of ham

FOR BREADING AND FRYING

- 2 eggs
- 30 g flour
- 50 ml natural mineral water
- 200 g breadcrumbs
- peanut oil

MOZZARELLA IN CARROZZA
FRIED MOZZARELLA SANDWICHES

Cut the mozzarella into thin slices and pat dry with kitchen roll. Lay out 2 slices of bread on a work surface and layer the mozzarella over the top, covering them. Arrange the anchovies on top of one of the slices and the ham on the other. Top off each sandwich with more slices of mozzarella and another slice of bread.
At this point, put the two sandwiches on top of one another and place a weight on top of them for around an hour.
Make a very liquid batter from the flour, eggs and water and add a pinch of salt. Blend the batter with a hand blender. Take the pressed sandwiches and remove the crusts. Cut the mozzarella in carrozza into different shapes to distinguish between the two fillings, namely triangles (by cutting diagonally across the slice of bread) and rectangles. Soak the sandwiches in the batter then press them into the breadcrumbs using your hands to coat them thoroughly. Fry in oil at 160 °C for at least 2 minutes on each side. Serve the mozzarella sandwiches hot with the filling melted.

INGREDIENTS FOR 4 PEOPLE

- 4 Romanesco artichokes
- 2 lemons
- salt
- peanut oil for frying

CARCIOFI ALLA GIUDIA
DEEP-FRIED JEWISH-STYLE ARTICHOKES

Use artichokes that are large and firm. Roman *Mammole* or *Cimarole* artichokes are perfect. Thoroughly clean the artichokes by removing the outer leaves. Using a small knife, clean the stalk vertically down to the base: strip away a little of the green part on the outside but leave the tender heart and the white of the stem. Try to leave the stem long and in one piece, if possible. Remove the outer leaves of the artichoke, which are the toughest, and cut off the tips of the other leaves following the shape of the artichoke. This age-old method, the so-called "*capatura*", or trimming of the artichokes, is the only secret to this apparently very simple dish.

If you are not able to follow the shape of the artichoke, you could remove the top with a single cut perpendicular to the stem at the end of the white portion of the leaves. Rub each artichoke with lemon, then rinse in water and lemon juice. Dry the artichokes well and then hold them by the stem and beat each bulb down on a surface, so that the leaves start to open up. Fry them in a pot that is tall enough to cook them standing upright. The oil at this stage should not be overly hot: 130 °C is perfect. Immerse each artichoke head down in the oil and, using cooking tongs or a kitchen fork, hold it down to cook for 5 minutes. After the first frying, set the artichokes face down on kitchen roll. As soon as they are lukewarm, gently open the flower, separating the petals. When you reach the heart of the artichoke, sprinkle it with salt and gently press its head down onto the work surface. Now, fry for a second time at 150 °C for 3-4 minutes. Add salt and serve piping hot.

INGREDIENTS FOR 12 SUPPLÌ

FOR THE TOMATO SAUCE

- 1 kg peeled tomatoes
- 150 g shallots
- salt
- extra-virgin olive oil
- 500 g risotto rice
- 5 g salt
- 1 glass of dry white wine
- 70 g butter
- 30 ml extra-virgin olive oil
- 200 g cherry tomatoes
- 30 basil leaves
- 250 g cow's milk mozzarella

FOR BREADING AND FRYING

- 5 eggs
- 100 g flour
- 100 ml natural mineral water
- 500 g breadcrumbs
- peanut oil

SUPPLÌ/ITALIAN FRIED RICE BALLS

Put all of the raw ingredients for the tomato sauce in a large saucepan. As soon as the sauce begins to boil, carefully blend everything using a hand blender, then leave to cook for another 20 minutes over a low heat. Toast the rice in a large saucepan with a pinch of salt until golden. Add the wine and stir slowly with a wooden spoon until it has evaporated.
Add the butter, oil and salt and continue to stir for another 5 minutes. At this point add the diced cherry tomatoes, the tomato sauce and the basil leaves. Cook for 10 minutes, then spread the rice out onto a steel or marble surface to cool. Ideally, leave the rice for 6-8 hours. If that is not possible, make sure that the rice has at least cooled to room temperature. Cut the mozzarella up into slices, then into sticks and finally into cubes of around 1 cm on each side.

When the tomato risotto is cool, press it into a small pastry cutter that is about 5 cm in diameter. This will leave you with several small piles of cooked rice of the same weight. Make a cavity in the centre of each pile and fill it with a couple of cubes of cheese. Cover the mozzarella-filled centre with more rice and shape the balls for frying. Put the eggs, the flour, a pinch of salt and water in a mixing bowl and blend with a hand blender. After shaping the rice balls with your hands, gently press the sides so they become a little elongated, then dip them first in the liquid batter and then in the breadcrumbs. Instead of using your hands, place the supplì in a tray full of breadcrumbs and shake it from side to side to finish breading them. This way the breadcrumb coating will be more even. Fry in oil at 160 °C for at least 6-8 minutes and serve piping hot.

INGREDIENTS FOR 10 TOMATOES

- 10 large round tomatoes
- 2 kg potatoes
- 500 g Arborio rice
- 200 g Parmigiano Reggiano (aged 24 months)
- 50 ml extra-virgin olive oil
- 50 ml white wine vinegar
- 10 basil leaves
- 2 sprigs of rosemary
- garlic
- salt and pepper

FOR THE TOMATO SAUCE

- 500 g peeled tomatoes
- 50 g shallots
- salt
- extra-virgin olive oil

POMODORO "AL RISO"/RICE-STUFFED TOMATOES

Cut the tops off the tomatoes near the stem, remove the pulp with a teaspoon and keep the "lids" and all the seeds and liquid from inside. Put all of the ingredients for the tomato sauce cold into a large saucepan, without sautéing them. As soon as the sauce begins to boil, blend it carefully with a hand blender. Cook for another 10 minutes on a low heat. Put the rice in a wide, heavy-based pan and cook until the grains of rice are very hot, but not fully browned. Add in the tomato sauce, olive oil, salt, black pepper and basil leaves and stir. The rice should not truly cook, just develop a richer flavour and start the cooking process for a few minutes. While this is happening, wash the potatoes, cut them into large pieces and let them soak in boiling water and vinegar for 2 minutes. Fill the tomatoes with the rice, which will have cooled by this point, and cover with the tomato "lids" that you set aside.
Put the tomatoes in a large oven tray surrounded by potatoes. Add a drizzle of oil, a sprinkling of salt, an unpeeled garlic clove and cook at 180 °C for 50 minutes.

INGREDIENTS FOR 4 PEOPLE

- 1 kg potatoes
- 200 g approx. soft white flour (Italian 00 flour)
- salt
- 100 g Parmigiano Reggiano

FOR THE TOMATO SAUCE

- 800 g peeled tomatoes
- 100 g shallots
- salt
- extra-virgin olive oil

GNOCCHI AL "SUGO FINTO"
GNOCCHI WITH FAUX MEAT SAUCE

Take old potatoes, preferably a white-fleshed variety, and wash. Steam or boil them in their skins. While they are still hot, peel and mash them with a potato ricer. Put all of the mashed potato on a lightly floured surface and start adding the flour. The quantity of the flour in this recipe is just an estimate: two handfuls of flour, amounting to 50 g more than the recommended quantity may be enough, it all depends on the type of potatoes you use and how you cook them. The important thing to remember is that the more flour you use, the heavier the dough – and the final result – will be, so try not to use too much. The dough is ready when it no longer sticks to your hands. At this point divide the dough into pieces and roll into cylinders about a finger's width in diameter. Use a sharp, non-serrated knife to cut pieces that are 2-3 cm in length. Sprinkle with a little flour and make an indent in each one, pressing it with your thumb against a pastry board or against the reverse side of a grater, or else score them with the tines of a fork. Put all of the ingredients for the tomato sauce in a large saucepan. There is no need to sauté them first. The flavour of the shallots should not be overbearing; they are there to add a little sweetness. As soon as the sauce begins to boil, carefully purée it all with a hand blender. Simmer for another 10 minutes over a low heat. Cook the gnocchi in plenty of water with a little salt for around 8 minutes, which is to say for at least a minute after they have risen to the surface. Add 3 spoonfuls of tomato sauce and the Parmigiano, and stir until creamy.

INGREDIENTS FOR 4/6 PEOPLE

- 500 g fresh egg lasagne sheets
- 400 g buffalo mozzarella
- 400 g "Vacche Rosse" Parmigiano Reggiano (aged 24 months)
- salt

FOR THE TOMATO SAUCE

- 800 g peeled tomatoes
- 100 g shallots
- salt
- extra-virgin olive oil

LASAGNE

Place the ingredients for the tomato sauce in a large saucepan. Cook all the ingredients together, without sautéing any of them. As soon as the sauce begins to boil, purée it all with a hand blender. Let it cook for another 10 minutes over a low heat. Carefully remove the mozzarella from its liquid, finely slice it and leave it in a colander to let the milk drain away. Leave for at least 30 minutes, then use your hands to tear the slices of mozzarella into small pieces and leave them to drain again in the colander. Take an oven dish, grease it, then start making layers with the tomato sauce, the rectangular sheets of the fresh pasta (as wide as the tray), the grated Parmigiano and the mozzarella. Add more layers until you have filled up the tray: 5-6 layers will suffice. Before putting it in the oven, spread a generous amount of cheese over the top layer, so that a crunchy, melted crust forms. Cook in the oven at 180 °C for at least 30 minutes. Grill for the last 5 minutes and serve warm or hot. It tastes delicious even at room temperature or the day after.

INGREDIENTS FOR 4/6 PEOPLE

- 3 kg aubergines
- 200 ml dry white wine
- 400 g buffalo mozzarella
- 400 g "Vacche Rosse" Parmigiano Reggiano (aged 24 months)
- basil
- salt
- black pepper

FOR THE TOMATO SAUCE

- 800 g peeled tomatoes
- 100 g shallots
- salt
- extra-virgin olive oil

PARMIGIANA DI MELANZANE
AUBERGINE PARMIGIANA

Wash and remove the stems from the aubergines, then cut them into slices, each barely 1 cm deep. Take care to slice the aubergine lengthways. Spread out the slices on a tray covered with a sheet of baking paper, without overlapping them. Spray some white wine on top. Use a spray bottle similar to the one you would use to water your plants and the wine will spread evenly and thoroughly across the aubergine slices. Season with pepper and salt and place in a hot oven (180 °C) for at least 15 minutes. Carefully remove the mozzarella from its liquid, slice it finely and leave it in a colander to let the milk drain away. Leave for at least 30 minutes, then tear the slices of mozzarella apart by hand, making small pieces, and return to the colander to allow the remaining milk to drain away. In the meantime, place all the ingredients for the tomato sauce into a large saucepan. There is no need to sauté them first. The flavour of the shallots should not be overbearing; they are there to add a little sweetness. As soon as the sauce begins to boil, carefully purée it all with a hand blender. Simmer for another 10 minutes over a low heat. As soon as the aubergines are cooked through, spread the tomato sauce over the bottom of a Pyrex or ceramic oven dish and start making layers by alternating aubergines, sauce, mozzarella, the grated Parmigiano and basil, creating at least 3 layers. Take care not to use too much sauce; spread a small ladleful between one layer and the next. Finish off with two ladles worth of sauce, and a generous amount of mozzarella and Parmigiano. Cook at 180 °C in the oven for at least 40 minutes. Finish under the grill for 2 minutes and serve warm, never hot.

INGREDIENTS FOR 4 PEOPLE

- 1 veal shank weighing approx. 1.5 kg
- 1 stick of celery
- 2 carrots
- 2 onions
- 1 clove of garlic
- 200 g soft white flour (Italian 00 flour)
- 100 ml dry white wine
- 100 ml vegetable stock
- 5 ml Worcestershire sauce
- 1 bay leaf
- extra-virgin olive oil
- salt and pepper

OSSOBUCO

Peel the garlic. Cut the celery, carrots and onions into small pieces. Place everything in a baking tray and cook with a drizzle of olive oil, the garlic clove and salt and black pepper in an extremely hot oven for 20 minutes. Have your butcher cut the pork shank into 3-4 cm thick slices. Dip the sliced veal shank in flour and brown in a sizzling frying pan. When the meat is well browned, add in the vegetables and bay leaf then deglaze with the white wine.
Cook over a low heat until the wine is fully reduced. Add the hot stock and cook in the oven at 180 °C for half an hour. When the meat is tender, the marrow will be soft and almost melting, and the vegetables will be almost overdone. Strain the sauce at this point and place the vegetables to one side. Purée the strained sauce, vegetables and Worcestershire sauce with a hand blender, and then strain again through a fine sieve. Serve the veal shanks with a generous amount of sauce on top.

INGREDIENTS FOR 6/8 PEOPLE

- 800 g minced beef
- 400 g Italian-style pork sausage meat
- 1 egg
- 50 g "Vacche Rosse" Parmigiano Reggiano (aged 24 months)
- 4 slices of white bread → *recipe on page 242*
- 50 ml whole milk
- 2 boiled potatoes
- 500 ml dry white wine
- 1 bunch of parsley
- nutmeg
- salt and pepper
- 300 g flour
- peanut oil for frying

POLPETTE AL VINO/MEATBALLS IN WINE

Mix the two types of meat with the black pepper, salt and a pinch of nutmeg. Chop the parsley, soak the bread without its crusts in milk, beat the egg and mash the boiled potatoes with a fork. Add all these ingredients and the Parmigiano to the meat mixture, then mix vigorously with your hands. Shape into small balls of about 50 g and coat them all over with a little flour. Fry at 130 °C for 30 seconds. Drain on kitchen towel, then place in a pan with a drizzle of olive oil and the white wine. Once the liquid starts to boil, let them cook for another 15 minutes. Serve hot.

THE CAFÉ

A new project that ranges from the cult of breakfast to the ritual of the aperitif.

THE DESIRE FOR SWEETNESS

Rethinking breakfast, light lunches, snacks and aperitifs, setting them in an innovative space. The Roscioli brothers' dream becomes a reality.

The Roscioli Caffè – Café Roscioli – opened its doors on 11th January 2016. The patisserie project took shape while this book was being written. When Pierluigi spoke to me about it for the first time, I thought that it was a contradiction, given that Alessandro and Pierluigi had both told me several times that they would never open another Roscioli venue. And yet contradictions are part of growth and with the closure of the historic Pasticceria Bernasconi, which was located just twenty metres away from the Delicatessen, despite scepticism and their apparent reluctance to growth and to proliferating the format, the decision to make it part of the "Roscioli system" was fairly predictable.

Pierluigi had been looking for a space for months, a plot or property into which he could extend the bakery's patisserie. When a neighbour told him about the imminent closure of Bernasconi, it seemed like it had all been planned out. To oversee the new project, Alessandro and Pierluigi called on a dear friend, Enrico Rusticali, a graphic designer and art director, with whom they had been dreaming of doing something together for years. Everything had to be conceived and there was a need for creativity within the Roscioli team.

Over six months of work and renovation, a minimalist and linear design by the Morq architectural studio, plus some clear and creative ideas, gave life to a threefold space: a café, a patisserie and a cocktail bar.

Sandy brown and lava black, day and night, chiaroscuro.

The café has a double soul: bright and luminous, with a long marble counter and the vibrant colours of the patisserie behind the glass cases in the first room; dark and shadowy in the second room, which features a single table around which people can sit to drink a cocktail while eating oysters, mixed nibbles, tasters and tapas. This is a place that makes coffee and cappuccinos by day, that serves pastries and leavened goods in the morning, but that, in the evening, transforms into a private and intimate haunt for foodies who gather around the single table.

Coffee reigns supreme in the first room, which features a manual machine that has been customised for various blends and therefore different pressure levels and temperatures. One of the machine's groups has a manual Neapolitan lever pump, while the other features a volumetric pump. For the entire water dispensing process both pumps maintain a constant pressure of 9.2 bars, unlike a standard lever machine. This shrewd thinking creates a pre-infusion system that extends the time that the water and the coffee are in contact, thereby ensuring that all the organoleptic qualities are extracted from the espresso as fully as possible. Only Arabica coffee is used every day for this extraction process, almost as if it were dogma, and only beans that are ground fresh. On rotation, depending on the season, year and moment, coffees from South America that have been selected, toasted and blended by Gianni Frasi are tasted – especially those from Guatemala, such as the coffee from the highlands of Huehuetenango – as well as a blend of three African Arabica coffees (Kenya, Ethiopia and a secret Arabica variety) with a pungent, primitive aroma and Indian coffees with interesting notes of acidity.

Salvo

Behind the café counter today stands Salvo, a young man from Piazza Dante in Naples who spent many years in the Delicatessen. His moustache and beard are his calling card and his astute and vibrant look welcomes whoever crosses the metal threshold of the patisserie to drink a coffee or a creamy cappuccino. After working in several restaurants, first in London and then at the Osteria dell'Arancio

in Grottammare in the Marche region, Salvo arrived at Roscioli as a sommelier in 2010. In the beginning the hectic rhythms of the Delicatessen and – more than anything else – the incredible number of covers, left him shaken and intimidated, but then all that frenzy became routine and turned into pure adrenalin. Salvo also nursed a passion for coffee alongside his passion for wine: he studied, deepened his understanding and took many workshops. The biodiversity in coffee beans is equal to that of wine and he found working on the aromas and scents interesting work with vast potential.

Other ways of making and drinking coffee were experimented with, alongside the classic espresso: infusion, siphon, Aeropress and Chemex coffee makers... plus teas, infusions and herbal preparations, and a wide range of single-origin honey, which would serve to enrich the range on offer. Speciality Coffee had finally arrived in Rome. A vast range of green coffee that had achieved over 80 points out of 100 during a tasting session, in accordance with the parameters of the SCAA (Specialty Coffee Association of America) would take their turn on the coffee menu, thereby expanding both horizons and tastes.

The patisserie is different to the one at the Antico Forno. Pierluigi and his lovely pastry staff have put aside the ring cakes and tarts from the bakery and have instead created a more sophisticated product range that takes tradition as a starting point but transforms it.

The idea is to have a large tray of little, contemporary pastries, that should be arranged as if they were mosaic tiles: arranged depending on the time of the day and emptied depending on the gluttonous desires of the clientele. The Roman Maritozzo buns are freshly filled with cream, as are the cornetti, which are filled in front of the clients. Charlottes and Monte Bianco cakes are displayed alongside shortcrust pastries, leavened goods, fruit tarts and little chocolates. When in season, colomba, panettone and pandoro cakes take over the shop. It is a kind of sweetness that has enriched the Roscioli universe: less homey, yet genuine, elegant and boasting great refinement.

In addition to the sweet counter, there are also several trays of savoury nibbles: sandwiches, braided bread, rolls and toasties. The Delicatessen, just 20 metres away, deals with the sandwiches, embellishing them with excellent products

from the Italian culinary world. The lobster in the lobster roll is freshly cooked, the bisque that features in several sandwiches has been prepared by Nabil with langoustine heads, the butter is French and the chicken in the club sandwich is cooked over a low temperature after marinating in honey.

The bread brought back from American by uncle Franco in his day has become a central part of the soft, gourmet finger sandwiches that come before an aperitif over the course of the day. That bread which had become poor and commercial over the course of almost fifty years is now gourmet once again and comes in different varieties prepared with various kinds of seeds and different flours.

A toast is called in the dark room at sunset, the list of wine and nibbles replaces the coffee menu and tastings come one after another.

Maria Elena, the youngest child of Rita and Marco, studies psychology and she has never worked at either the bakery or the Delicatessen. When I ask her if she will ever take over the Antico Forno Roscioli, she says that throughout all the years they have always kept her far away from the family business, almost protected. Both Alessandro and Pierluigi insist that everything they are building will not be taken on by the family. After all is said and done, they believe that the future of their "little sister" and their children should be different from their past, which is heavy with sacrifices. Fortunately, contradictions and transformations are part of this family story and perhaps a son for a chef, a daughter for a manager or a sister able to fall in love with a project built with such passion, in the end, could turn the tables.

Roscioli ®
caffè
PASTICCERIA

INGREDIENTS FOR APPROXIMATELY 40 CASTAGNOLE

- 500 ml natural mineral water
- 150 g butter
- 400 g soft white flour (Italian 00 flour)
- 10 eggs
- 2 g salt
- butter for greasing
- peanut oil for frying
- icing sugar for dusting

CASTAGNOLE/SWEET DOUGH BALLS

Melt the butter into the water in a saucepan, taking care to mix well. As soon as the liquid begins to boil, remove the saucepan from the heat, add in the flour and stir vigorously. The success of this recipe lies entirely in this delicate step, from when the mixture thickens to when it detaches from the pan. Return the saucepan to the hob and cook for about 5 minutes over a low heat. There are a few tricks to knowing when the choux pastry is ready: touch the dough and see if it is firm, listen for a slight frying noise and notice the dry white residue that slowly begins to form on the walls of the saucepan. Turn off the heat, move the dough into the planetary mixer and allow it to cool. Once the dough is merely warm, mix on a medium setting until smooth. Add in the eggs, the salt and gently beat them in. Take a sheet of baking paper and lightly grease it. Using a pastry bag with a medium-sized, plain nozzle, create balls around 2-3 cm in diameter. Wet your finger and press down gently on the top of each ball, flattening the top a little. Take a deep frying pan, heat the oil to 180 °C and fry the dough balls by dipping the baking paper containing all the *castagnole* into the boiling oil. The baking paper will detach by itself within a few seconds. Remove it quickly with tongs, turn the dough balls and cook until they have turned a nice, even golden colour. Remove the excess oil from the dough balls and leave them to dry on kitchen roll. Fill them with cream by piercing the bottom with a pastry bag. Dust with icing sugar and serve.

INGREDIENTS FOR APPROXIMATELY 30 MARITOZZI

- 1 kg of strong flour
- 500 ml natural mineral water
- 130 g of margarine
- 130 g granulated sugar
- 20 g fresh brewer's yeast
- 3 eggs
- 10 g salt
- zest of 1 lemon
- 1 vanilla pod

FOR THE FROSTING

- 1 egg white
- 100 g icing sugar
- 40 ml natural mineral water
- 5 drops of lemon juice
- whipped cream for decoration
- icing sugar

MARITOZZI CON LA PANNA
SWEET BUNS FILLED WITH WHIPPED CREAM

Pour the flour into the planetary mixer and add the water slowly. When the water has mixed in well, add in all the other ingredients until the dough is even and elastic. Move it to a large bowl, cover it with cling film and leave to rest in the fridge at 5 °C for 24 hours. Remove the cling film and turn the bowl over on a flat, greased surface. Separate the dough into round balls around 60-70 g in weight. Knead each ball individually, pressing down lightly at the ends to make slight oval shapes. Cover with a slightly damp cloth and allow the *maritozzi* to rise until they have almost doubled in size. Bake at 200 °C for 15 minutes, making sure that the buns are pale on the edges and slightly brown on top.
The measurements for this recipe are for two baking trays of *maritozzi*. Bake them separately to get the best result. Whisk the egg white together with the sugar and lemon. Slowly add in the water and mix it all together. Place over a low heat and cook for 5 minutes, mixing the whole time. Turn off the heat and leave to cool. Brush the *maritozzi* while they are still hot, but not just out of the oven. Wait for the buns to cool down, then cut them down the middle and open them slightly. Fill the spaces you have created with a generous amount of whipped cream, sprinkled with a little icing sugar.
To make *maritozzi* for lent, add 100 g of rum soaked raisins, 100 g candied orange pieces and 100 g lightly toasted pine nuts into the dough before you divide it up. This kind of *maritozzi* is usually served without whipped cream.

INGREDIENTI PER 20 BOMBE

- 500 g strong flour
- 150 g whole milk
- 125 g eggs (3 eggs)
- 75 g butter
- 15 g fresh brewer's yeast
- 10 g lime honey or acacia honey
- 3 g salt
- 500 g custard *
- peanut oil for frying
- sugar for decoration

BOMBE
CUSTARD-FILLED DOUGHNUTS

Dissolve the brewer's yeast in the milk, add in 2 tablespoons of flour, then mix and leave to rise for about half an hour. Cut the butter into pieces and leave it to soften at room temperature. Whisk the eggs. Knead the risen dough with the rest of the flour, the eggs and the salt in a planetary mixer and blend together on the lowest power setting. Take the cut butter and blend thoroughly until the dough is extremely elastic. Leave it to rise for 2-3 hours. Lightly flour a pastry board and roll out the dough so that it is around 2 cm thick. Use a dough cutter to create discs and leave them to rise again until they have almost doubled in size. The *bombe* are ready to be cooked when the peanut oil gets to 160 °C. Drain them from the oil, remove any excess with kitchen paper and roll in the granulated sugar. Use a pastry bag with a small, plain nozzle to fill the *bombe* and serve.

* CUSTARD

- 800 ml whole milk
- 200 ml fresh cream
- 400 g sugar
- 300 g egg yolk
- 40 g rice starch
- 40 g corn starch
- 1 vanilla pod
- 1/2 orange peel

Mix the egg yolk and sugar together in a small bowl. Once the mixture starts to thicken and become lighter in colour, add in the sifted starches and enough cold milk to dilute it, beating out any lumps to obtain a silky, creamy consistency. Open the vanilla pod with a sharp knife and remove the seeds. Warm up the rest of the milk with the open vanilla pod, the vanilla seeds and the orange peel in a deep saucepan. Just before it begins to boil, turn off the heat and wait for the milk to cool. Strain the milk to remove the vanilla pod and orange peel and pour it over the flour, egg, and sugar mixture. Mix together well and then pour it into a saucepan once again. Cook over a low heat for about 3 minutes, until the cream is thick and firm. Pour the custard mixture out into a bowl, leave it to cool and then cover with cling film, with the film touching the custard. Place in the fridge and allow to cool for at least a couple of hours.

INGREDIENTS FOR 6 PEOPLE

FOR THE SPONGE FINGERS

- 150 g egg whites
- 235 g granulated sugar
- 130 g egg yolk
- 35 g acacia honey
- 75 g potato starch
- 170 g soft white flour (Italian 00 flour)
- 30 g icing sugar

FOR THE VANILLA MOUSSE

- 250 ml whole milk
- 100 g granulated sugar
- 4 egg yolks
- 15 g Isinglass (gelatine)
- 1 l fresh cream
- 1 vanilla pod

FOR THE RASPBERRY GANACHE

- 100 g raspberries
- 100 g white chocolate

FOR THE DECORATION

- 300 g strawberries
- 200 g raspberries
- 1 tbsp of icing sugar
- whipped cream

CHARLOTTE

Whisk the egg whites together with 185 g sugar. Heat the mixture in a pot, a deep one if possible, to 40 °C, then pour all of it into the planetary mixer and beat the mixture until it turns clear (not hard like a meringue, slightly softer).
Add in the egg yolks, the honey, the flour and the sifted potato starch and gently mix it all together with a spatula, not in the planetary mixer. Line a tray with baking paper, put the mixture in a pastry bag fitted with a small, plain 1 cm nozzle and pipe out sponge fingers around 8 cm in length. Spread out the sponge fingers well on the tray, dust the two types of sugar over the top and bake at 200 °C for 5 minutes. Open the oven for 1 minute, close again and allow to bake until the sponge fingers are done (2-3 minutes). They should not turn golden in colour, instead they should be light yellow. Once baked, set them to one side and leave to cool. If you want to, you can leave them to dry out for at least two days. Beat the egg yolks with the sugar to create the base for the mousse. Warm up the milk with the vanilla seeds without bringing it to the boil, then pour it into the egg yolks and sugar. Soak the isinglass and, once soft, add it to the custard. Place the custard in the saucepan and cook over a low heat (do not heat above 82 °C) until it begins to thicken. Once it has thickened, turn off the heat and leave to cool. Whip the fresh cream and add it to the custard mixture. Wash the strawberries, then dry and slice them. Melt the white chocolate in a bain-marie and put to one side. Wash and blend the raspberries, then strain the pulp through a sieve to get a raspberry coulis. Carefully mix the coulis with the white chocolate. Take a circular, spring-form cake tin at least 10 cm deep, with the spring unclasped, and arrange the sponge fingers in a sunburst pattern on the bottom and vertically around the sides to encase the cake. Pour the mousse over the sponge fingers and spread the ganache on top with a spatula, before adding the fruit. Add a second layer on top of the strawberry pieces, starting with the sponge fingers and finishing off with the mousse. Cut the sponge fingers to size or leave them whole, long and round, if you prefer. Compact the ring and place the tin in the freezer for a couple of hours. Remove the Charlotte cake from the freezer an hour before serving, leave at room temperature for 5 minutes and then remove the cake tin ring and decorate with the whipped cream and raspberries and dust with icing sugar.

INGREDIENTS FOR 6 PEOPLE

FOR THE MERINGUE

300 g egg whites

300 g sugar

FOR THE WHIPPED CREAM

500 ml fresh cream

30 g icing sugar

FOR THE CHESTNUT PURÉE

500 g candied chestnut pieces

80 g butter

FOR THE DECORATION

1 candied chestnut

icing sugar

unsweetened cocoa powder

MONTE BIANCO

Whisk the room-temperature egg whites together with the sugar. Heat the mixture in a saucepan, preferably one with a thick bottom, and heat the egg whites together with the sugar to 40 °C. At this point, pour everything into the planetary mixer and whisk until the meringue is stiff. Take a sheet of baking paper and form 4 cm tufts of meringue with a pastry bag fitted with a plain nozzle. Bake at 100 °C for around 6 hours. Take the candied chestnuts and pass them through a potato ricer and mix with butter. You will get a soft, firm purée. Whisk the cream together with the sugar and fill a pastry bag fitted with a ridged nozzle. Take a serving dish or use individual cupcake liners and build up alternate layers of whipped cream, meringue and the candied chestnut purée. Try to create a dome shape, adding up to three layers of whipped cream, meringue and chestnut purée. Compact the dome with a spatula, then add some "spaghetti" of candied chestnut on the top. Finish off with tuffs of whipped cream, meringues dusted with cocoa powder, place a candied chestnut in the centre and sprinkle it with icing sugar.

INGREDIENTS FOR 1 CLUB SANDWICH

- 3 slices of white bread (2 cm thick) *
- 50 g guanciale (cured pork cheek)
- 80 g honey-roasted chicken
- 60 g mayonnaise
- 30 g BBQ sauce
- 5 drops of Angostura bitters
- 1 Beefsteak tomato (Costoluto or Cuore di Bue variety)
- 1 egg
- 1/2 head of lettuce
- 50 g salted French butter
- fresh thyme
- salt

CLUB SANDWICH

Toast the slices of guanciale in a non-stick pan, remove the excess oil with kitchen towel without tearing them and leave to cool. Slice the tomatoes half a centimetre thick and season with oil and salt at least half an hour before making the sandwich. Toast one of the three slices of bread (the two outer slices should be soft) and butter it on the top and bottom. Make a sauce using the mayonnaise, the Angostura bitters and the BBQ sauce. Begin to stack the sandwich, placing the non-toasted slice first. Spread the sauce, then add the lettuce, the crunchy guanciale, the thinly sliced pieces of chicken, the thyme and the tomato. Stack the toasted slice that has been buttered on both sides and continue upwards, layering the sauce, the lettuce, the guanciale and a fried egg. Add the last slice of bread with the sauce already spread on it. Gently cut the sandwich in half. If it helps, place a wooden toothpick in each triangle, which is the traditional way to serve it.

* WHITE BREAD

FOR THE BIGA (PRE-FERMENTED BREAD STARTER)

- 1 kg soft white flour (Italian 00 flour)
- 550 ml natural mineral water
- 1 g fresh brewer's yeast

- 1 kg of biga
- 100 g soft white flour (Italian 00 flour)
- 600 ml natural mineral water
- 20 g honey
- 20 g salt
- 100 ml extra-virgin olive oil
- 10 g brewer's yeast

Combine all the ingredients for the biga sponge in the kneading machine and knead on the lowest setting for 10 minutes. Cover with a linen cloth and leave to rest at room temperature for 12-14 hours. When the biga sponge has doubled in size, start by slowly kneading it for 4 minutes on speed setting 1, then more energetically for 6 minutes (speed setting 2). Add flour and water and knead vigorously to develop the gluten in the dough. Add in the rest of the ingredients, including the yeast dissolved in a little water and knead until you get a smooth, elastic dough. Leave it to rest for 10-15 minutes, then divide the dough into pieces that are the same size as your bread tins. Butter and flour the tin, place a piece of dough in each tin, pressing down to fill the corners. Leave them to rise until the dough reaches the edges of the tin, then cover with a lid and bake at 220 °C for 40 minutes. You can also add sunflower and pumpkin seeds to the dough when it is almost ready (before you divide it up).

INGREDIENTS FOR 1 ROLL

- 1 olive oil roll *
- 200 g Romanesco courgette
- peanut oil
- 75 g cider vinegar
- 150 g cow's milk mozzarella
- extra-virgin olive oil
- salt
- black pepper

PANINO CON LA CONCIA
ROLL WITH FRIED COURGETTE

Cut the courgettes, making sure not to slice them too finely, and fry in peanut oil until light brown. Remove excess oil with kitchen roll and leave to cool. Once cooled, season with salt, pepper, vinegar, and olive oil and place in the fridge for at least one night. Construct the sandwich by placing a couple of thick slices of mozzarella and the seasoned zucchini inside.

* OLIVE OIL ROLLS

FOR ABOUT 10 ROLLS OR 25 MINI-ROLLS

FOR THE BIGA (PRE-FERMENTED BREAD STARTER)

- 1 kg soft white flour (Italian 00 flour)
- 550 ml natural mineral water
- 1 g fresh brewer's yeast

- 1 kg biga
- 1250 g soft white flour (Italian 00 flour)
- 125 g of margarine
- 25 g salt
- 6 g fresh brewer's yeast
- 500 ml natural mineral water

Vigorously knead the yeast, the flour and the warm water together to make the biga. Stretch the ball vigorously to help strengthen its gluten structure. Leave to rise for 12 hours. Place 1 kg of the risen biga sponge in the kneading machine, add in all the other ingredients and knead on a low speed for 10-15 minutes. The dough will become firm but not overly hard. Turn it over on a work surface, form a ball and leave it to rise at room temperature for 30 minutes. Break up the dough into pieces that are about 50 g each (or 20-25 g if you are making small rolls) and shape the most even balls you can. Technically speaking, this is when we are rounding off the buns, i.e. when we turn the dough ball quickly in the hollow of our palms to create pieces that are almost perfectly spherical. If you need to make longer rolls, shape dough balls first, then lengthen them to your liking. Place the buns on a tray lined with a piece of baking paper and leave them to rise for at least 40 minutes, placing a damp cloth on top. With long rolls, place them in a tray next to one another. With hamburger buns, use your fingers to flatten each one and make holes with a roller. If you don't have one, pierce the buns all over with a fork. Depending on your tastes, you can add seeds or brush the rolls with beaten egg. Cook at 260 °C for 6-7 minutes, placing a bowl of water at the bottom of the oven if possible.

INGREDIENTI PER 1 PANINO

- 80 g finely cut veal brisket
- 1 long olive oil roll
  → *recipe page 245*
- 1/2 head of lettuce (heart)
- 1 Beefsteak tomato (Costoluto or Cuore di Bue variety)
- 50 ml extra-virgin olive oil
- 40 g mayonnaise *
- 10 g traditional wholegrain mustard
- lemon juice
- salt

PANINO CON PETTO DI VITELLA ALLA FORNARA
VEAL BRISKET SANDWICH "ALLA FORNARA"

Slice the tomatoes and save all of the juice. Marinate them lightly in oil with a sprinkling of salt and let them sit for 10 minutes. Dress the lettuce heart with a few drops of lemon juice. Mix the mayonnaise and the mustard together in a bowl. Season to taste with salt or adjust the acidity with a drop of lemon. Steam the bread and begin to stack it. Spread the bread with the mustard-mayonnaise sauce, layer the pieces of seasoned lettuce heart, the finely cut veal brisket and the tomato slices. Add some more sauce and a few drops of the tomato juice and serve.

* MAYONNAISE

- 3 egg yolks + 1 whole egg
- 1 l sunflower oil
- 1 tbsp of white wine vinegar
- 1 tbsp of lemon juice
- salt

Make sure that all of the ingredients (and the bowl of the planetary mixer) are cold, right from the fridge. Begin beating the eggs slowly. When they have been thoroughly whisked and mixed, start to pour in the oil and increase the speed.
When the mayonnaise is mixed well, add in the vinegar, lemon juice and salt. Keep whisking for another 30 seconds and refrigerate.

* VEAL BRISKET

- 1.5 kg veal brisket
- crushed sage, rosemary, garlic (1 clove)
- coarse salt and pepper
- 50 ml dry white wine
- 1 carrot and 1 celery stick
- 2 bay leaves
- extra-virgin olive oil

Prepare a seasoning of crushed rosemary, sage and garlic (without its core). Add the coarse salt and ground pepper to the mortar. Remove the excess fat from the meat and grease it evenly with a few tablespoons of oil. Keep massaging the meat, adding the mixed seasoning, then place it in a lightly greased baking tray, along with the chopped carrots, the celery and the bay leaves. Cook in the oven at 160 °C for about three hours. Once upon a time, this recipe was made by taking advantage of the heat from the baker's oven.
The meat was placed in the oven at dinnertime, when the bakery closed its doors, and was taken out at midnight, when the bakery would open once again to bake its bread for the next day. With this in mind, consider that the lower the temperature you cook it at, the more delicious the meat will be. As it cooks, gradually add in the white wine, as required; the meat should always be wet and moist. Once cooked, remove from the oven and set to one side.

INGREDIENTS FOR 1 SANDWICH

- 2 artichokes "alla cafona" *
- 2 slices of white bread → *recipe page 242*
- 80 g tuna in olive oil
- 40 g mayonnaise → *recipe page 247*
- tabasco sauce, oregano

FOR THE BISQUE

- 3 langoustine heads
- 1/2 celery stick and 1/2 carrot
- 1 shallot
- 1/2 clove of garlic
- 1 tomato
- 50 ml dry white wine
- parsley, thyme
- salt and pepper

TRAMEZZINO CON TONNO E CARCIOFINI
TUNA AND ARTICHOKE SANDWICH

To prepare the bisque, sauté the shallot, half a clove of garlic and the sliced celery and the carrot. As soon at the shallot begins to brown, add in the langoustine heads and toast them well, pressing them down on the bottom of the pan. Add the white wine and simmer until it reduces. Next, add in the salt and pepper, sliced tomatoes, aromatic herbs and enough water to cover the langoustine heads and the vegetables by a few centimetres. Simmer for half an hour until the bisque has reduced by half. At this point, strain and filter it and place it back into the pot and let it reduce some more. When the texture becomes creamy, it's ready. Leave it to cool and then combine it with the mayonnaise. The mayonnaise should be double the amount of the langoustine bisque. Carefully mix in two drops of tabasco sauce. You will get an intense pink coloured sauce. Mash the tuna with a potato masher and cut the artichokes into wedges. Spread the pink sauce on the slices of bread, followed by the tuna and artichokes and sprinkle with oregano, then cut into triangles and serve.

* ARTICHOKES "ALLA CAFONA"

Rome and Romanesco artichokes have a close and enduring relationship. In the Roman cookbook, *De re coquinaria* (On the Subject of Cooking), Marcus Gavius Apicius talks about hearts of *cynara* boiled in water and wine, for which Romans were known to have a particularly voracious appetite. The Romanesco artichoke is big and features a (flower) head that is hard and compact, and a long, thick stalk. It is often entirely free from thorns and bristles on the inside. One of the first products tasted when the Delicatessen opened was an artichoke preserved in olive oil that perfectly conveyed the taste, but above all the crunchiness, of the Romanesco artichoke. They were quickly "adopted" and today they continue to be one of the flagship products. The producer selects artichokes exclusively from the Pontine Marshes in the Lazio region, specifically the area near the town of Sezze. Picked in April, the artichokes are cleaned by hand with a knife and soaked in a water, vinegar, wine and salt solution. Then they are cooked for 20-30 minutes, in order to get to the heart of the artichoke and drained. A centrifuge is used to remove most of the water that the artichokes absorbed when being boiled. They are then left to rest for about 2 hours. Once dried to the right point, the artichokes are ready to be placed in a glass jar, seasoned with lesser calamint and covered in oil.

INGREDIENTS

- 1 lobster
- 1 long olive oil roll
  → *recipe page 245*
- 60 g mayonnaise
  → *recipe page 246*
- 30 g BBQ sauce
- 5 drops of Angostura bitters
- 1 teaspoon of Traditional Balsamic Vinegar of Modena
- 50 g salted butter
- 50 g mixed wild-leaf salad
- 1 lemon
- extra-virgin olive oil
- fine salt
- pepper
- coarse salt
- extra-virgin olive oil

LOBSTER ROLL

Boil the water in a large pot with two handfuls of coarse salt. The water should be well-salted to establish both the flavour and colour of the lobster. Dip the live lobster head down into the pot and cook without a lid for about 6-7 minutes. The top shell will turn a bright red colour. One cooked, remove from the water and place to one side. While it is still warm, cut the top shell and remove the meat, including the claw meat. Make a sauce using the mayonnaise, the Angostura bitters and the BBQ sauce.

Steam the roll to warm it up and spread the inside with melted butter. Dress the mixed wild-leaf salad with oil, vinegar and a pinch of salt. Construct the roll with the sauce, the mixed wild-leaf salad, the sliced lobster meat and drizzle the melted butter over the top to finish. If you fancy, adding some lemon zest at the end is a nice touch.

RECIPES LIST

OTHER RECIPES

FARNESE

Stefano Bonilli had thought about writing the story of the Roscioli family and its bakery for a long time. At the beginning of 2014, with the collaboration of the publisher, the shape and structure of the book were more or less established. The first photo shoot took place with photographer Maurizio Camagna, then Stefano's premature passing suddenly interrupted the project.
Today this book has taken shape once again. The work was not done using the few notes that Stefano left behind, but rather was drawn from the many hours we spent together over the years. From the endless conversations on journalism, writing, food and the restaurant world that we engaged in while strolling across the cobbles found in this corner of Rome, which he had chosen as his refuge, or sitting in the piazza where he would drink his frothy cappuccino every morning while reading the paper.
At first we thought that we would have to weave and embellish the words of his published articles and his reviews together with the notes spread across his many tablets and computers. Then we realised that writing a book as Bonilli would have done was an impossible task. We came to this realisation because he was also trying to find the way to tell the story of this family of bread makers that he had seen bloom into life and with whom he had shared so much. Stefano was looking for a way, in other words, that he had still not entirely figured out.
A year has passed. It was in the autumn of last year that we looked for the way to tell the story of this family that we first explored through a series of interviews, then as friends because, as happens when you tell a story with a certain closeness, friendships blossom.
An original story has been created, giving particular attention to the details, to the story, to the people and to the beauty that are essentially the result of a journey that we have taken together with Stefano.

E.M.